P9-CAU-561

The Hottest Stars of
YouTube, Instagram,
Twitter, and Vine

BACKSTAGE

Social Media Stars

PASS

Mark Damian

TRIUMPH
BOOKS

Copyright © 2014 by Triumph Books LLC

No part of this publication may be reproduced, stored in a retrieval system, or transmitted in any form by any means, electronic, mechanical, photocopying, or otherwise, without the prior written permission of the publisher, Triumph Books LLC, 814 North Franklin Street, Chicago, Illinois 60610.

This book is available in quantity at special discounts for your group or organization. For further information, contact:

Triumph Books LLC
814 North Franklin Street
Chicago, Illinois 60610
(312) 337-0747
www.triumphbooks.com

Printed in U.S.A.

ISBN: 978-1-62937-089-7

Content developed and packaged by Rockett Media, Inc.
Written by Mark Damian
Edited by Bob Baker
Design and page production by Patricia Frey

Photographs courtesy of Getty Images unless otherwise noted.

This book is not authorized, approved, or endorsed by the entertainers included herein or any organization or entity associated with or affiliated with these entertainers. It is not an official publication.

CONTENTS

CHAPTER ONE

CYBERSPACE PIONEERS

If Generation X was the MTV Generation, then Millennials and Generation Z are surely the Internet Generation — and probably more specifically, the YouTube Generation.

For anyone who's been hiding under a rock, there now exists a new brand of professional celebrity (most of them very young) who make their living (sometimes quite lucratively) mainly by recording and posting videos of themselves on YouTube, supported by other social media such as Facebook, Twitter, Instagram and Vine.

The following book takes a look at some of the names and faces making their way in the new social media landscape today, and brings you closer to a phenomenon that is changing the way we view the definition of celebrity.

Justin Bieber comes immediately to mind.

Probably the foremost exemplar of social media's star-launching potential, Bieber, now a household name, was plucked from virtual obscurity and transformed practically overnight into an online sensation, and then, in short order, into a real world superstar whose face has become a ubiquitous sight on television and magazine covers. His name has become a synonym for "teen idol" and all that the phrase implies, both positive and negative. Legions of "Beliebers" managed to make Bieber the first artist to have seven songs from a debut record to chart on the Billboard Hot 100. To date, no one has parlayed social media stardom into near-iconic status quite the way he has.

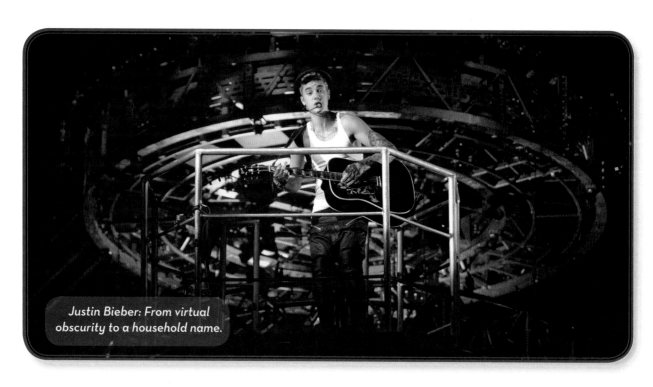

Justin Bieber: From virtual obscurity to a household name.

"I would go on the iTunes chart and see the hottest songs, then I'd cover them. People would go on YouTube and search for those songs. That's how I got my views. I'd post two or three songs a week."
—Austin Mahone

Rosanna Pansino poses with
one of the fans that have
propelled many to stardom

Another prime example is Austin Mahone, whose rise to pop stardom began with the singer, then 13 years old, posting videos on YouTube. Austin was quoted in *Details* magazine describing his homemade business model for gaining exposure: "I would go on the iTunes chart and see the hottest songs, then I'd cover them. People would go on YouTube and search for those songs. That's how I got my views. I'd post two or three songs a week." These posts included one of himself (with a full set of gleaming braces still on his teeth) crooning a cover of Justin Bieber's "Mistletoe" which led to a recording deal with Chase/Universal Republic Records worth a reported seven figures. In 2013, Mahone was named an Artist To Watch by the MTV Video Music Awards for his fourth single, "What About Love," and on April 27, 2014, the day of its release, his EP *The Secret* rocketed past albums by Coldplay and Mariah Carey to claim the number one spot on iTunes. With the braces finally off, Austin now packs the star power to shut down malls and pack venues across the country with throngs of tween-aged "Mahomies," to whom Austin credits his meteoric rise and who are acknowledged as being one of

> # SOCIAL MEDIA STARS KNOW THAT IF IT WERE NOT FOR THE FANS, THEY WOULD NOT BE WHERE THEY ARE TODAY.

the most active and engaged fan bases across all of social media.

Certainly not everyone who posts a video of themselves on YouTube becomes star, but there have been many who made their mark early on in social media, and whose names and faces, at least for a time, became buzzwords on talk shows and in school hallways across America.

Here are a few you might remember:

BROOKE ALLISON BRODACK – Known by her YouTube name "Brookers," she has the distinction of being dubbed by *The New Yorker* as "the first real YouTube star" and was named a "Crossover Star" by the *Wall Street Journal* on its New Media Power List on July 29, 2006. Her video "Chips," a spoof sketch that suspensefully portrays Brooke psyching herself up to take on a potato chip bag's challenge to "eat just one," was cited by *Entertainment Weekly* as one of the "great moments in YouTube history." Brookers was the first female ever to reach the number-one subscribed YouTube spot, and her videos have garnered 49 million views to date.

LUCAS CRUIKSHANK — This young comedic actor initially brought his character Fred Figglehorn to viewers through his YouTube channel. Cruikshank's hyperactive, digitally altered Figglehorn voice, which sounds like a high-pitched cartoonish chipmunk, has been heard by over a billion viewers on YouTube alone. By April 2009, Cruikshank's channel became the first YouTube channel to reach one million subscribers (and would become the third to reach two million), making it the most subscribed channel on YouTube at the time. The character went on to spawn a Nickelodeon franchise and has generated three feature films, music videos, two recorded albums, a television show and several online programs, including four seasons of his original Fred series and an animated series called "It's Fred!" Cruikshank describes his content as "programming for kids by kids."

RYAN HIGA — Higa's comedy clips, posted under the name Nigahiga, have attracted 12 million subscribers. (Incidentally, Higa's clips are cited by Austin Mahone as the inspiration behind his first YouTube postings, which depicted Austin and his school friend Ryan Constancio horsing around at Constancio's parents' house.) Higa's content includes character sketches, popular movie parodies, spoofs on advertisements and how-to videos. He and video partner Sean Fujiyoshi currently provide the starring voices

RYAN HIGA

Lucas Cruikshank:
YouTube's Fred Figglehorn

Chris Crocker is well known for his
"Leave Britney Alone" videos.

for a Nickelodeon anime series called "California Rollers."

CHRIS CROCKER — Who can forget the flamboyant, gender-bending young man whose histrionic "Leave Britney Alone" videos were discussed on news shows across the world after they went viral in the blink of a mascara-streaked eye? It then went on to be parodied on *South Park*, and *Wired* magazine named it the top video of 2007. "Leave Britney Alone (Part 2)" remains YouTube's second most discussed video of all time across every category, with more than 350,000 posted comments. The video's predecessor, "Leave Britney Alone pt. 1," posted on MySpace, also garnered 35 million views and half a million comments.

JUDSON LAIPPLY — Known primarily for a single viral video, his "Evolution of Dance" clip, which depicted Laipply dancing to excerpts from 32 popular songs, propelled him to YouTube's number one spot in 2006, receiving 70 million views in less than eight months. At the height of its popularity, it was rated as the Number One Most Viewed Video of All Time, the Top Rated Video and the Most Discussed Video on YouTube.

TOBY TURNER — Posting under the name Tobuscus, this comedian,

JUDSON LAIPPLY

SOCIAL MEDIA PLATFORMS HAVE ALREADY PROVED A VIABLE SPRINGBOARD TO STARDOM FOR A NUMBER OF NOTABLE FIGURES.

musician and self-described "viral marketer" has gained a total of over 14.1 million subscribers and 2.9 billion video views over his three YouTube channels as of April 7, 2014. His online spoofing and sketch comedy has received mainstream recognition on CBS News and *Wired* magazine. Turner also voices the character of Neville on the Cartoon Network's animated series *The High Fructose Adventures of Annoying Orange.*

JOHN "JACK" PATRICK DOUGLAS — Under the username jacksfilms, comedian and internet personality Jack Douglas has attracted over a million subscribers and 100 million views with humorous videos such as "The WTF Blanket (Snuggie Parody)", which alone has had nearly 21.5 million views to date. He has collaborated frequently with Tobuscus under the name Tobjacksus, and his 75-installment series "Your Grammar Sucks," in which he pokes fun at fan-submitted examples of incorrect grammar, spelling and punctuation from internet comments sections, has been featured on *Huffington Post.*

RAY WILLIAM JOHNSON — Johnson became famous for his YouTube show "Equals Three," in which Johnson, using a format similar to

AP IMAGES

that of television's *Talk Soup* and *Tosh.0*, provides humorous commentary on viral videos. With 10.7 million subscribers and 2.4 billion views, Johnson's is the 12th most subscribed YouTube channel.

BENNY AND RAFI FINE — Considered pioneers of online video, The Fine Brothers have produced hundreds of videos since 2004. Their channel TheFineBros has drawn over 8 million subscribers and more than 1 billion views since the brothers began posting online clips in the earliest days of YouTube. They have collaborated with many of the best-known YouTubers over the years, including PewDiePie, Shane Dawson, Connor Franta, Zoella and Smosh. They are known for their popular Reaction videos (Kids React, Teens React, YouTubers React, Elders React), which won a special Emmy Award for "Best Viral Video Series"

Benny and Rafi Fine, with the cast of "Kids React"

at the 39th Daytime Emmy Awards in 2012, and recently teamed up with Nick Cannon to produce a television show for Nickelodeon based on the Kids and Teens React series.

SMOSH — Anthony Padilla and Ian Hecox collectively comprise the extremely popular YouTube comedy duo Smosh. A mix of comedy sketches, vlogs, viewer challenges and lip synch videos, Smosh has been the Number One Most Subscribed Channel on three separate occasions since 2006, and was voted the "All-Time Favorite Most

PEWDIEPIE

Subscribed YouTube Channel" in the YouTube Wiki Polls. The duo currently has over 17 million subscribers and has posted more than 300 videos on YouTube.

PEWDIEPIE — This roster would not be complete without acknowledging Swedish YouTuber Felix Arvid Ulf Kjelberg, known to millions by the moniker PewDiePie. With 27.5 million subscribers, PewDiePie, whose Let's Play channel consists largely of video game playthroughs accompanied by Kjelberg's often humorous running commentary, currently holds the number one spot on YouTube and is the Most Subscribed YouTube Channel of All Time. In June of 2014, *Forbes* magazine and the *Wall Street Journal* reported that Kjelberg currently rakes in over $4 million in ad sales a year, most of which is pure profit. PewDiePie is also ranked as the number-one subscriber gainer on YouTube by VidStatsX, gaining an average of one subscriber every minute.

According to VidStatsX, PewDiePie and Smosh are the only two all-original content channels generated by an individual or duo ranked in the top 10 categories of both Most Subscribed and Most Viewed. Other Most Subscribed

> **THE POWER OF SOCIAL MEDIA TO TURN YOUTUBERS INTO BANKABLE BETS IS CLEARLY SOMETHING THAT CAN'T BE IGNORED.**

channels include broad general categories such as Gaming, Music, Sports and News, and Most Viewed consist primarily of VEVO music channels for individual popular recording artists like Rihanna and Eminem (and, perhaps as the ultimate crossover testament, Justin Bieber).

No social media figures have achieved Bieber's level of stardom as of this writing, but odds are excellent that more will, further proving that the power of social media to turn YouTubers into bankable bets is clearly something that can't be ignored. @

CHAPTER TWO

E-MALE: TODAY'S SOCIAL MEDIA SENSATIONS

CONNOR
FRANTA

The Generation Z and Millennial audience that propelled Justin Bieber to prominence is continually engaged in the ongoing process of selecting its newest heartthrob. Views, subscribers, and thumbs-ups count as votes in the online election process. But what qualities do you need to be a social media star?

Without a doubt, good looks don't hurt. Judging from the top male stars, swoosh-y hair helps, too.

But surely there's more to YouTube success than a cute face and swoosh-y hair?

British vlogger and radio personality Dan Howell (known to millions by his screenname *danisnotonfire*) might have best summed up the appeal of YouTubers with this simple remark in an interview with the *Huffington Post*: "Vloggers on YouTube are in the business of personality."

Humor, style and honesty attract viewers, as well as sharing real-life stories and opinions that audiences can appreciate.

Here are some faces who, by virtue of the millions of social media fans they draw each day, count among the most popular:

CONNOR FRANTA

Fan favorite Connor Franta is a social media star whose visibility has spread like wildfire. At 21, Connor was the oldest member of the YouTube "supergroup" channel Our2ndLife (O2L), which also features Kian Lawley, Sam Pottorff, JC Caylen, Trevor Moran and Ricky Dillon. His recent departure from the group resulted in an outpouring of grief, but don't count Franta out yet. As he stated in his final O2L post, he isn't going

> ## "I LIKE TO THINK THAT I COME ACROSS AS A REALLY HAPPY, POSITIVE PERSON. BUT THAT'S NOT ALWAYS THE CASE."
>
> **—CONNOR FRANTA**

anywhere, and will continue to vlog on his own YouTube channel and keep his dedicated fans informed of his doings via social media.

In fact, if wallpapering social media sites with hundreds of apple-cheeked selfies were a sure route to global domination, Connor Franta would be ruling the world by now.

He hit 2 million subscribers on his personal YouTube channel in April, 2014, and he gained over another million subscribers during his time on the O2L collab channel.

Born in Wisconsin, Connor moved to a small town in Minnesota as a child. Connor is the second youngest child of four siblings — two older brothers, Dustin and Brandon, and a younger sister, Nicola. He was on the swim team in high school, and had a job at a pool center where he worked as a life guard and swim instructor.

On Connor's eighteenth birthday, September 12, 2010, he posted his first public YouTube video, titled "A HARRY POTTER BIRTHDAY," in which he pretended to be an 11-year-old receiving his acceptance letter to Hogwarts School of Wizardry and Witchcraft and shows off a magic wand he had ordered from the Harry Potter theme park in Orlando,

giving it a test run complete with special effects.

In 2011, Connor began attending Saint John's University in Minnesota, where he competed in varsity swimming and diving.

Over the next four years Connor also used several social media platforms to promote two busy YouTube channels (ConnorFranta and More Connor) on which he posted hundreds of vlogs documenting his life and sharing entertaining anecdotes with a growing subscriber base.

In July 2012, he joined the new collab project Our2ndLife featuring the current members, as well as Ricardo Ordieres, who later left the channel to work in radio. He uploaded many more videos on his personal O2L channel and also on the group channel. O2L soon became YouTube's biggest collab channel with over 2.3 million subscribers. In October 2013, when Connor's main channel hit a million subscribers, he celebrated by filming himself jumping into a swimming pool naked and performing various gags and stunts.

Connor was one of the biggest attractions of this year's DigiTour, and his appearances at events like VidCon drew throngs of fans who showed up while it

Connor Franta at DigiFest NYC with Ricky Dillon and JC Caylen.

was still dark out just to secure a place in line, and then waited for seven hours to see Connor and O2L. In "YouTubers Behind Closed Doors" he professed his gratitude to the fans who put so much into these gatherings, and also the sense that it all felt a bit "unreal."

With such a rigorous schedule and this degree of adulation, it's easy to see how someone who started out vlogging in his parents' living room might be feeling overwhelmed. In "How YouTubers Act Off Camera" he says, "A lot of my life is spent with and revolves around YouTubers. You only see a portion of my life," and he admits that he has a different persona in real life than is seen in his public vlogs.

After a month-long tour of the U.S. with DigiTour, immediately followed by the madness that is VidCon filled

O2L performs onstage at DigiFest NYC at Citi Field

with meet-and-greets, main stage events, panels, and photo sessions, Connor confessed in a vlog titled "I AM DEAD" that he was exhilarated but also exhausted. This was perhaps a foreshadowing of the announcement that was soon to come.

On July 7, 2014, Connor addressed the O2L audience in a serious video called "A New Chapter" with the news that this video would be his last for the channel, as he was leaving the group. He explained that he had been "a very unhappy person for the past six months," and that he felt his content had been lacking in "creativity and depth" during this time, asserting, "I'm not okay with that."

"I like to think that I come across as a really happy, positive, in general well put-together person. But that's not always the case," he said, echoing previously expressed sentiments. "To you guys, it may seem that way all the time because you only see portions of my life — the good portions, really. It's not always that way. It's not always good. I'm just a person, and I struggle a lot with a lot of things."

He stated that O2L, which had been a huge part of his life for nearly two years, had started to feel too much like work, which was something he never intended it to be. But he assured viewers that being part of O2L was one of the most wonderful experiences of his life, and that he bears only love and good wishes for the rest of O2L, who would remain his close friends, and that "nothing will, ever, I repeat EVER, change that." He also urged O2L fans to disregard any negative gossip or rumors that might crop up in the wake of his departure concerning his relationships

with Ricky, Trevor, Kian, Sam and JC, who he considers his family. "And because of that," he said, "I do not want to stick with this channel and tear it down by not having my heart fully in it."

Connor further revealed that he had been dealing with some personal issues, saying, "I have a lot going on in my life. I have a lot going on with YouTube, I have a lot going on with my friends, I have a lot going on with my family, I have a lot of personal things I'm dealing with behind the camera."

He stated that he has always been someone who does things to make other people happy, but that the decision to focus on his personal channel was one he felt he had to make for himself: "I'm not the kid who was making videos in his bedroom for fun four years ago. I hate that. It puts such a bad taste in my mouth. And because of this, I am so overwhelmed... Something needs to change if I want to keep doing this."

He concluded by insisting that he wasn't going anywhere and would continue to be present on YouTube, Twitter and Instagram, hopefully investing his work with more quality and substance than he had been able to do in recent months.

Connor's last O2L video received over 2 million views and generated over 72,000 comments, many of them expressing sadness from fans, but also an outpouring of support for Connor and good wishes in his future endeavors, including support from all of the remaining O2L members.

JOEY GRACEFFA

The following could be a recipe for Joey Graceffa:

1 pair of long-lashed, ocean-green eyes

baby-faced expressions (to taste)

*aerodynamic hair
(werewolf-y amounts of it)*

1 mouthful of blindingly white teeth

a dash of parody

a pinch of sarcasm

several silly fake accents

2 seasons on The Amazing Race

1 sweet, bubbly personality

Add 3.3 million YouTube subscribers, 237 million views, collabs with practically everyone and a major Hollywood deal. Stir. Bake for 23 years, and serve extremely hot. Enjoy!

Joey Graceffa is a vlogger, gamer, actor, singer, model, comedian, producer,

Hunger Games and One Direction fan, reality game show contestant, and internet personality who often adds the suffix "-anya" to various words and closes his vlog posts with the *Hunger Games* motto, "May the odds be ever in your favor."

The odds certainly seem to be favoring this experienced social media star, whose brand of slightly daffy comedy and sweet vulnerability has been endearing him to his fans for nearly a third of his young life.

Despite not being able to name four animals that start with the letter C or four states that start with the letter W while standing under a cold shower [see Joey's collab vid with British YouTuber Marcus Butler titled "TWO BOYS GET WET CHALLENGE"], Joey clearly knows what his fans like. Joey has found his way into so many impressionable hearts that when he attends VidCon, he is greeted by a crowd of hundreds screaming their lungs out.

Born in Massachusetts, Joseph Michael Graceffa began his YouTube career at age sixteen, posting videos with his best friend Brittany Joyal under the screen name *WinterSpringPro*. The sketch comedy videos they made throughout high school gained them a

JOEY

growing number of subscribers. They netted millions of views, which led to Joey being made a YouTube partner, and allowing him to make money from his videos.

He later split off to produce his own YouTube channel under the name JoeyGraceffa. Under his new moniker he recorded a number of frank, inspirational videos, including his "Draw My Life" post, which has received nearly 5 million views. In it, he recounts his personal struggles growing up in an unstable home, including his mother's problems with alcoholism and his own difficulties in school with bullying and a learning disability caused by ingesting lead paint when he was six.

Through a steady stream of vlog posts, Joey has traced his journey from East Coast to West Coast, and from Special Education student to social media star. He recalls that from the time he entered school until he was a sophomore, he spent half of each school day in special education classes, a fact he tried hard to hide from his friends at the time. Joey tried to sneak from his regular classes to his special ed classes without being seen. He remembers going home in tears, wanting to be like everyone else, and that's a feeling that has never

changed. By seventh grade, he felt he no longer needed the extra help provided by special education, but his parents disagreed. From that point on, he set a goal to prove his parents wrong and get out of the special education before graduation. Working as hard as he could over the next two-and-a-half years, he succeeded in joining the regular curriculum by tenth grade, where he kept striving and managed to excel, even getting into honors classes his junior and senior years.

Hoping to major in film after graduating from Marlborough High School, he applied to his dream school, Emerson College, and was rejected twice. For a time he attended what he refers to as a "crusty state school" where he was miserable, but he continued making and posting YouTube videos and building an increasing fan base. At 19, he curtailed his formal education and moved to Los Angeles to follow his dream of being an actor, and that's where his YouTube career has continued to flourish.

Joey has been roommates with several other popular YouTubers, including Anthony Padilla (*Smosh*), Kalel (*KalelKitten*) and Sawyer Hartman. He now lives with Amazing Race partner

Megan (*Strawburry17*) and her younger brother David (*dayvideo*).

He is a notable collaborator with practically every popular YouTube personality, including Sawyer Hartman, Tyler Oakley, Justine Ezarik, Miranda Sings, Zoe Sugg, Alfie Deyes, and Marcus Butler. One of his most frequent collabs is with Shane Dawson, whose videos with Joey are known as "Shoey."

Graceffa has stated that being a professional YouTuber has been a full-time paying job for him since age 18. Prior to that he did a summer stint stocking ice cream trucks (a job that his father's girlfriend secured for him), and then worked scooping ice cream and making sundaes in a restaurant. His last job before becoming a full-time YouTuber was a retail position at an Abercrombie & Fitch store.

In the early days of Joey's YouTube partnership, his WinterSpringPro channel with Brittany Joyal went from bringing the team around $100 a month to $400-$800 a month in a short time.

"It adds up," Joyal told a local journalist from their hometown of Marlborough, Massachusetts back in 2009. (The article lists Joey as a freshman majoring in film at Fitchberg

JOEY HAS GAINED AN AVERAGE OF ONE NEW SUBSCRIBER EVERY 10 SECONDS TO HIS YOUTUBE CHANNEL.

State College at the time — presumably the "crusty state school" he was too polite to name.) "We're constantly getting paid and we don't even know it. We get paid 24/7."

They soon signed a contract for a line of merchandise that included T-shirts, hats and tote bags, and that was only the beginning.

In August 2012, Joey was cast as a contestant on CBS' *The Amazing Race*, although he kept the news under wraps until filming was completed that December, disclosing on YouTube with team partner Megan Camarena

how they had traveled to Bora Bora, Scotland, Vietnam, Bali, New Zealand, Botswana, Berlin and Washington, DC during the previous five weeks recording the show, set to be aired that spring. The pair was the season's youngest team and came in 5th place. They returned to the show in February 2014 for *The Amazing Race All-Star Edition* where they finished 9th.

In October 2013, it was revealed in a video by another YouTuber that Joey's federal tax return for that year reported his income at over $200,000, much of it presumably from the proceeds of his YouTube work — although the story of the events leading up to this revelation is perhaps more entertaining than the revelation itself.

A few days prior to the disclosure, Graceffa had parked his car in a Los Angeles neighborhood while visiting his YouTube producer Stacey Hinojosa (*StacyPlays*) to record a Minecraft playthrough video for his gaming channel. Upon going to retrieve his car, Graceffa found it had been towed. He immediately posted a vlog titled "STOLEN CAR!" in which he admitted to blocking someone's driveway, but only by "a tiny bit." He went on to admonish the neighbor for having him towed. And he recalled leaving his federal tax return on the passenger's seat.

Unbeknownst to Joey, the person whose driveway he blocked is a Los Angeles comedian named Nate Clark who has a YouTube channel of his own. On it, he posted a rebuttal to Joey's vlog in which he showed a photo of Joey's blue Toyota Prius blocking the entire width of his driveway before it was towed. He also decided to get a bit of revenge by disclosing Joey's tax return information. The response video drew almost 3.3 million views, receiving thousands of comments in support of Clark, but also thousands of angry comments from enraged Joey Graceffa fans.

The controversial incident may not have shown Joey at his best, but it hasn't hurt him. His popularity continues to grow by leaps and bounds.

Joey's visibility has increased significantly since 2013, and his bankability has grown along with it.

Since December 2013, Joey's main channel has been partnered with StyleHaul, the YouTube multi-channel network with a focus on style and fashion. He was previously partnered with Defy Media (formerly Alloy Digital), for whom he co-hosted the company's online series *Teen.com* with *Amazing Race* partner Meghan Camarena. His dedicated gaming channel JoeyGraceffaGames remains partnered with Defy.

Joey also created and starred in the 2013 webseries *Storytellers*, which he funded through a Kickstarter campaign that raised over $140,000. Joey described the show as *Skins* meets *Are You Afraid of the Dark?*, mixing coming-of-age stories with comedic horror.

Judging from the comments of his fiercely devoted and protective fans, there are many who find Joey's story inspirational, and who find Joey a likable, watchable, engaging personality. One of his strengths is that he manages to come across as honest and sweet and disarmingly genuine.

In May of this year, Joey signed with United Talent Agency, a major Hollywood talent agency, which also represents YouTubers Shane Dawson, iJustine and Bethany Mota. Joey will work with UTA "to capitalize on his massive online following to create opportunities in film and television acting, publishing, touring, and music — all while maintaining his relationship with his 1.2 million Twitter fans and YouTube following."

THE BRITS — YOUTUBE IN THE UK

British YouTubers frequently collaborate with their American counterparts, but they definitely have a scene of their own. They have their own events (Summer In The City, co-organized by YouTuber Tom Burns), a charity web-a-thon called Stickaid (founded by YouTuber Myles Dyer), and the early YouTube scene in the UK is colorfully documented in a 12-part webseries called "Becoming YouTube" by UK writer, filmmaker and vlogger Benjamin Cook on his channel ninebrassmonkeys.

Here are some of the personalities who make up today's British Invasion in social media:

DAN HOWELL

Known by the screen name *danisnotonfire*, 23-year-old Daniel James Howell is the left-handed half of the award-winning BBC radio and online team Dan and Phil, but he is also a highly visible YouTube star in his own right.

In his "Draw My Life" video, Dan tells how, as a child, he expressed an early interest in theater, which his parents encouraged. This led him to pursue acting and playing the piano. He participated in local theater productions of *West Side Story, Romeo and Juliet* and *Fame.* When he was 17, he decided to give up his dream of acting in a moment of self-doubt that he says is one of his only regrets in life.

With college approaching, Dan planned to study law and become a barrister, figuring this course would render him more employable than his hopes of becoming an actor. However, he decided to forego college for a few semesters and take a "gap year" before entering university, and it was during this time he began posting his first YouTube videos.

He had been following other vloggers on YouTube for three years, citing Shane Dawson, Charlie McDonnell (*charlieissocoollike*) and the Community Channel as influences. At the suggestion of friends, including Phil Lester who would later become his professional partner and roommate, he uploaded his first YouTube video, titled "Hello Internet," on October 16, 2009. This was followed by semi-regular postings in which Dan gave updates about his life.

Dan Howell with Phil Lester at BBC Radio 1 Teen Awards

Dan has blogged about vlogging for the *Huffington Post* UK edition, and can be seen discussing different aspects of being a YouTube celebrity in Benjamin Cook's online series "Becoming YouTube." In 2011 and 2012, he took part in "Stickaid," a charity that raises money for UNICEF. He also won *Sugarscape's* "Hottest Lads of 2012" competition, and placed first runner up the next year, coming in second to his friend and co-host Phil Lester.

Fans can purchase merchandise featuring the Danosaur — a cartoon drawing of Dan dressed in a *Where The Wild Things Are*-like dinosaur suit, with a dialog bubble that says, "RAWR!"

Dan's YouTube channel has over 3.5 million subscribers and over 200 million views.

CASPAR LEE

Caspar Lee is a 20-year-old South African YouTuber who frequently collaborates with the UK YouTube contingent and posts his own vlogs under his latest channel simply titled *Caspar*. Caspar rose to YouTube prominence under his previous channel DiCasp, which is short for "Director Caspar."

As Caspar tells in his "Draw My Life" video, he was born in London, and his family moved to South Africa when he was very young. He spent his early years in a rural area called Fort Nottingham with a small population and few opportunities for making friends. His family moved again, this time to Durbin, one of South Africa's biggest cities, where he attended an all-boys school. When he was 11, the Lees relocated yet again to a holiday town on the Western Cape of South Africa, which he hated at first because there wasn't a lot to do, although it got better for him when he started playing tennis and making new friends.

Around this time, his parents got divorced, which was a traumatic event for Caspar, although they both eventually found happiness in second marriages, and Caspar has spoken very fondly about both of his stepparents in his videos.

Caspar began posting humorous videos on YouTube in 2011 when he was 16. He had two unsuccessful YouTube channels during his first year of posting, after which he created the channel *DiCasp*, with which he would become well known in the YouTube community.

His early videos, which sometimes featured his sister, Theodora; his mother, Emily; and his dog, Summer; began to gain a following in his own country.

Caspar Lee
and Nick Hissom

In 2012, he took a trip to London that played an instrumental role in his life. During his stay there, he made collaboration videos with more established YouTubers including *Jacksgap* brothers Jack and Finn Harries, Alfie Deyes, Marcus Butler, and Bertie Gilbert (*bertiebertg*). Links provided in these videos brought Caspar to the attention of a wider audience, and in a short time his base grew dramatically. He returned to South Africa to finish high school and, inspired by his London experience, posted a video titled "Pro YouTuber" in which he asserted his resolution to return to England and forge a career as a professional YouTuber.

On New Year's Eve 2012, he boarded a flight back to London and, 13 days later, moved into a flat with Alfie Deyes from the YouTube channel PointlessBlog. He continued to make videos, collaborate and meet the British YouTube community. Living in London allowed him, in his own words, "to work with some of the best YouTubers in the world on a daily basis."

Caspar's channel has featured first-time interviews with many of his YouTuber friends including Jack and Finn Harries, Jack Devine, Joe Sugg, Dan Howard, Tyler Oakley and fellow

Caspar worked with Jack and Finn Harries (Jaskgap) while in London.

South African YouTuber Troye Sivan. His separate interviews with the Harries brothers have had over 2.5 million views each.

He is currently roommates with Joe Sugg, creator of the YouTube channel ThatcherJoe and brother of YouTube star Zoe Sugg (*Zoella*).

In the two years since publicly stating his aspiration to become a YouTube figure, Caspar has gained 2.5 million subscribers, is a member of the as-yet unrealized music project called Youtube Boyband which also features Alfie Deyes, Marcus Butler, Joe Sugg and Jim Chapman, and while visiting America to appear at this year's VidCon, he and the rest of the YouTube Brits were swarmed by eager fans.

He recently completed filming on *Spud 3: Learning to Fly*, the second sequel of the hit South African film series in which he will be playing the character Garlic alongside fellow South African Troye Sivan, who has played the title character in all of the *Spud* movies. The film's own YouTube channel lists Caspar as "South Africa's most successful YouTube star" and cites the power of online video to present successful vloggers with new opportunities to make it onto the big screen. The movie also stars Monty Python legend John Cleese and is scheduled to be released later this year.

TROYE SIVAN

Troye Sivan Mellet, better known as Troye Sivan, is the 19-year-old YouTube musician and vlogger who was seen portraying the young James Howlett, a.k.a. Logan, a.k.a. Wolverine, in the 2009 *X-Men* movie *X-Men Origins: Wolverine*. Troye was born in Johannesburg,

South Africa. Two years later, his family relocated to Australia.

As a child, Troye landed the lead in the musical *Oliver!* at Perth's Regal Theater, a role that allowed him to show off his musical talents publicly. Over the next three years he also performed several songs on charity telethons, and made it to the grand finals of *Star Search 2007*.

The same year he also began uploading his first YouTube videos under the screenname *TroyeSivan18*, which included a recording of him singing a song by Declan Galbraith. A Hollywood agent from the William Morris Agency was doing a Google search for Galbraith and stumbled upon Troye's video instead, and he was impressed. He got in touch with Troye by email and asked to have his parents contact him, which lead to Troye having an agent.

His big break came in 2009 when 13-year-old Troye was cast as the teenager who would become Wolverine in the blockbuster movie *X-Men Origins: Wolverine*. Again, the internet proved instrumental in Troye's career. He had filmed an audition for the part on his computer at home in Perth, which he sent via email to his manager, who then sent it to an agent, who sent it to the film's casting director, who in turn

Troye Sivan and Oli White at DigiFest LA.

elite boarding school for boys. *Spud* was a hit in South Africa and was nominated for six South African Film and Television Awards, including a nod for Troye for Best Lead Actor in a Feature Film. It went on to spawn a successful 2013 sequel titled *Spud 2: The Madness Continues*. Troye was joined by South African YouTuber Caspar Lee in the franchise's third film, *Spud 3: Learning to Fly*, which recently completed principal photography and is set to be released in South Africa later this year.

In May 2011, Troye began writing a song called "The Fault in Our Stars" inspired by the John Green novel. He recorded it in his bedroom using an electronic keyboard that he didn't know how to play, and posted the unfinished work, along with lyrics on Tumblr. The song received over 100,000 notes literally overnight. Encouraged by the response and suggestions that he film a music video of the song, Troye made a trip to Princess Margaret Hospital for Children in Perth to shoot on location for a day.

The result is a moving video, posted to YouTube on May 5, 2013, that depicts children in the cancer ward where Troye spent the day filming, and focuses particularly on two teenage girls, Kimberly and Montana, both of

sent it to director Gavin Hood. After three weeks of anxiously waiting, the secretary at his school pulled him out of science class and brought him to the principal's office, where his family was waiting to give him the good news.

A starring film role followed in 2010, when Sivan was cast as the title character in the first of the popular South African *Spud* movies. In the series, Troye stars alongside Monty Python legend John Cleese in a coming of age story set at an whom had lost their hair from cancer treatments and are seen smiling into the camera, showing off One Direction t-shirts and pillowcases, and watching videos of themselves made in the hospital that day with Troye. (Kimberly had been an active YouTuber and Tweeter for several years prior to being diagnosed with cancer, and links to both girls' social media sites were given in the video. Sadly, on December 5, 2013 Kimberly's mother announced on Kimberly's Twitter feed that Kimberly had lost her battle with cancer, and thanked the many people who had shown support for Kimberly over social media.)

The song was available for purchase on Bandcamp and iTunes, with 100% of the proceeds going to benefit the oncology center at Princess Margaret Hospital for Children. The video went viral, attracting over 3.5 million views on YouTube.

John Green recounted in his Tumblr feed that a crew member on the set of the film *The Fault in Our Stars* approached him around that time and said, "I loved your book, but I really loved that song about your book by the Australian guy Troye." Green went on to recommend the song to his audience and remarked on what a magical week it had

been and what a gift Troye had given him and the children at PMHC.

On August 7, 2013, Troye revealed that he is gay to his YouTube audience in a vlog called "Coming Out," three years after coming out to his family. In the video he cites being inspired by other coming-out stories on YouTube, and says that he has received widespread support from his friends and his devoted fanbase.

On the first day of VidCon 2014, Troye Sivan announced to screaming fans the advance release of his new album, titled "Trxye." He also disclosed on his YouTube channel that he had signed a recording deal with Universal Records on his birthday one year earlier, a development he chose to keep under wraps until the record was finished. The album is a five-song EP with the song "Happy Little Pill" issued as the first single, and corresponding music video expected to follow.

"I've spent the last year working with the most incredible producers and writers in the most incredible places," Troye told YouTube viewers. "I wrote over 40 songs and it has been the most intense and insane journey."

Catch more from Troye Sivan on the big screen and social media sites everywhere. @

CROSSOVER
FROM THE LAPTOP TO THE BIG SCREEN AND BACK AGAIN

For some, social media success is an end in itself. For others, the goal all along has been to use social media as a means of breaking into traditional media.

Perhaps the most obvious transition from social media to traditional media is in reality television, where social media stars can introduce themselves to TV audiences while continuing to be themselves. Many YouTubers have experience in this area: Phil Lester appeared on *The Weakest Link;* Joey Graceffa and Megan Camrena competed on two seasons of *The Amazing Race;* Girl group Fifth Harmony, who appeared at DigiFest 2014, was initially formed on *The X Factor;* and Frankie Grande (YouTube personality and brother of singer Ariana Grande) is finishing up a season on the show's American version.

Conversely, many established mainstream stars — including household-name celebs such as Madonna, Amy Poehler, Ashton Kutcher and former NBA star Shaquille O'Neal — are taking to the internet to produce new content expressly for online audiences. The medium offers them greater control and the ability to bring their vision to their audience without the influence of studio executives.

Actor, producer and crossover impresario Brian Robbins has had a hand in a number of successful online-to-television ventures, including *Fred: The Movie,* starring Lucas Cruikshank as his YouTube character Fred Figglehorn. When it premiered on Nickelodeon in 2010, it attracted 7.6 million viewers and became the highest-rated basic cable movie of the year among viewers ages 2 to 11, and went on to spawn two television film sequels and a regular TV series.

Robbins is also the founder of AwesomenessTV, a YouTube channel, which has had significant crossover success on Nickelodeon with a mix of style programing, sketch comedy and game shows featuring Joey Graceffa, Connor Franta, Jenn MacAllister and Andrea Russett.

There has been a recent flurry of big-money investment from mainstream studios in YouTube-native media. Last year, Dreamworks Animation purchased AwesomenessTV in a deal worth up to $117 million, which seems a steal in comparison to The Walt Disney Company's recent acquisition of Maker Studios (which produces Epic Rap Battles of History and, under the company's subsidiary Polaris, Felix Kjelberg's PewDiePie) for nearly $1 billion. Time Warner Inc. has been rumored to have a similar deal under consideration to acquire Fullscreen, the multi-channel network created by YouTube Partner Program co-founder George Strompolos, which provides marketing and management support for content creators like Shane

Dawson, Grace Helbig and The Fine Bros, all of whom are currently at work on television projects.

Other crossover projects have included *Camp Takota*, a big screen comedy about going back to summer camp, which starred YouTubers Grace Helbig, Hannah Hart and Mamrie Hart (a sequel is in the works). And Harley Morenstein recently took his *Epic Meal Time* format to A&E with a 16-episode series called "Epic Meal Empire."

Taking to the small screen in April, the boys from O2L along with other social media personalities supplied red-carpet coverage for the MTV Movie Awards, although Fullscreen manager Andrew Graham remarked that O2L doesn't see TV or recording music as a next step. For O2L, as for many digital stars, sticking to one medium isn't the point — rather, their goal is to become a multiplatform force. "In any way you can program or commercialize an individual brand, that's what they want to be," he told *Adweek*'s Michelle Castillo, with online video remaining at the core of those ambitions.

But other social media figures are less enthusiastic about transitioning to mainstream media. Aware of what they'd be giving up in making the jump to television or the big screen, many are content making a comfortable living serving their fanbase from their kitchens and sofas.

With her usual earthy candor, YouTube celeb Jenna Marbles expressed her satisfaction with "staying native" in an August cover-story interview with *Variety*: "Everyone is expecting you to use what you're currently doing on YouTube to do something else. I'm like, what's wrong with hanging out and making silly videos? It's not that I don't have the foresight for a larger project. I'm just not convinced it's worthwhile. [...] I really like existing on the internet, and I

The most obvious transition from social media to traditional media is in reality television.

like the community, I like the interaction of it. I like being my own boss."

Nevertheless, there remains an increasing degree of crossover between social media and mainstream media, especially with the entrance of agents, managers and producers into the social media sphere. Now, with the growing potential to turn a profit on platforms like YouTube and Instagram, traditional media and social media are merging forces every day.

In journalist Benjamin Cook's engaging webseries *Becoming YouTube*, John Green speculated that television and YouTube may not continue as distinct entities in the future. "I think that they are running toward each other, and like two cars headed at each other very quickly, that they are going to hit head on, and then they will become one very strange looking car that, at least initially, isn't particularly good at driving. But I do think that it will level out the playing field a little bit."

With all the new interactions between social and mainstream media taking the stage, it will be interesting to see what a blend of the old and new platforms will bring. ★

CHAPTER THREE

NET RETURN: GIRL POWERED

You Tube

Bethany Mota,
Michelle Phan and
Rosanna Pansino
attend the Unleash
YouTube Event and
Fan Meet-Up.

Female social media stars used to be a bit of a rarity, but many talented young women have managed to turn the odds in their favor and triumph spectacularly in what was once largely a boys' club.

To mention just some of them: Hannah Hart, Justine Erziak (*iJustine*), Grace Helbig (*DailyGrace*), GloZell Green, Roasanna Pansino, Colleen Ballinger (who performs as the popular "psycho-soprano" singing alter-ego character "Miranda" on her Miranda Sings channel, and vlogs about her real life on a separate channel), Meghan Camrena (*Strawburry17*), Shanna Malcolm (*HeyYoShanna*), Hazel Hayes, Tanya Burr, sisters Elle Fowler (*AllThatGlitters21*) and Blair Fowler (*juicystar07*), Carrie Hope Fletcher, Louise Watson (*SprinkleofGlitter*), Andrea Russett (*GETTOxFABxFOREVER*), Jenn McAllister (*jennxpenn*), Meredith Foster (*Silababe09*), Natalie Tran, Bunny Meyer (*Grav3yardgirl*), Ingrid Nilsen (*Missglamorazzi*), and Rebecca Black.

Here's a closer look at a handful of young women who are helping to refine the definition of social media success:

BETHANY MOTA

This entrepreneurial 18-year-old social media superstar has taken the internet by storm under the mantle of her YouTube channel macbarbie07, which she started when she was only 13. Mota is one social media celeb who has used internet stardom as a launching pad into the world of big business, specifically in the beauty and style markets.

Growing up in the small town of Los Banos, California, where the nearest shopping mall was an hour away (not surprisingly, internet shopping became an early feature in her life), Bethany was home schooled for long segments of her elementary and high school education. She also attended public school for three years, where she made friends and joined a cheerleading squad.

In middle school, Bethany was bullied by a former school friend who began to torment her through the very medium that would, ironically, soon send her rocketing to teen stardom. In her "Draw My Life" and "Strength In Numbers" videos, Bethany recounted that a classmate created a fake MySpace page in her name and filled it with cruel comments, leading to months of depression and anxiety attacks that caused her to withdraw from social activity.

It was during this period of isolation that Bethany discovered YouTube and the online style community. She began watching and posting videos as a way of trying to escape the stress of cyberbullying, and told *Business Insider* that YouTube "was kind of an outlet for me to be myself and not really worry about what anyone thought."

Being herself has since garnered Bethany over 6 million YouTube subscribers, plus more Instagram followers than *Vogue*, *Elle*, *Marie Claire*, *Glamour* and *Cosmopolitan* combined. A

SOCIAL MEDIA NOTORIETY DOESN'T TRANSLATE TO FINANCIAL SUCCESS FOR EVERY YOUTUBER.

video tour of her room has gained over 8 million views, and this June, Lifetime announced that Bethany would serve as a guest judge on Season 13 of *Project Runway*.

Social media notoriety doesn't translate into financial success for every YouTuber, but Mota has monetized her fame shockingly well. Mota nets an estimated $40,000 every month from YouTube ad revenue alone. Add it up — that's almost half a million dollars a year, just from posting short clips in her bedroom with practically no overhead (she still lives at home with her parents, and her first video was recorded with her camera propped on a pile of books because she didn't own a tripod).

She does not present herself as a pampered, spoiled diva who takes her good fortune for granted, or as someone whose life is unattainable and remote from her audience. Her brand of style is easy and attainable — she describes it as "bohemian, laid-back, free-spirited, girly and very comfortable" — and Bethany comes across as upbeat, energetic, genuinely nice and down-to-earth. (*Business Insider* called her "a virtuoso of positivity.") More importantly, she seems accessible: her avidly-watched "hauls"

BETHANY

— videos where she shares fashion finds from recent shopping expeditions — do not depict thousand-dollar Manolo Blahnik sling-backs or limited-edition Hermés Birkin bags; many of her things are from Target, H&M and JCPenney, items most of her viewers can actually afford to buy for themselves.

Meleina McCann, a 15-year-old from Oakland, said this about Bethany's appeal to *Business Insider*: "She's super sweet and so relatable. Her videos are so personal. It feels like she's speaking to me."

Bethany's own transformation is also inspirational. With the help of her social media "Mota-vators," she has moved light years beyond those days of being confined to her room in a state of bullying-induced panic. Now, when she walks through a mall, she induces waves of panic in thrilled fans who are breathless to see her and for the chance to get a selfie with their online fashion hero.

Mota's blend of business and wholesome, homespun style has been a boon not only for her, but also for

retailers eager to tap into her sprawling fanbase. "It's the perfect marriage of two of GenY's favorite things: technology and shopping," said Mike Boylson, chief marketing officer at JCPenney, in a 2010 *Los Angeles Times* article.

"The brand exposure is huge," said Kirstin Nagle, marketing manager at L.A.-based Forever 21 in the same article. "That's what makes it exciting for us."

Forever 21 and other companies are shifting some marketing power to consumers by partnering with haulers like Bethany to host shopping sprees and provide products to viewers in contests and give-aways. Last year, Bethany also signed a deal with Aeropostale, which now produces a Bethany Mota-branded jewelry and clothing line.

Bethany stresses, however, that integrity is important to her and that she is not a shill for businesses to co-opt as a branding opportunity. She retains creative control over her Aeropostale line, and has never accepted money from a retailer for making a video. When she does receive freebies, she discloses them under Federal Trade Commission rules. She told the *Los Angeles Times*, "I don't say yes to every company because...I don't want to recommend a product to my viewers if I don't believe in it."

Bethany was one of three content creators (along with Michelle Phan and baking vlogger Rosanna Pansino) featured in YouTube's first-ever advertising campaign, which appeared on TV channels like The CW and ABC Family, in magazines such as *Allure* and *Seventeen*, and across New York City and Chicago subway banners. The ads featured a smiling Bethany accompanied by the slogans "Fight Bullies with Style" and "Make Confidence THE Must-Have Accessory."

"I really want the base of my channel to be about inner beauty, and still feeling confident when you don't have makeup on and you're not all glammed up," says Bethany in her YouTube ad, summing up the prime objective that anchors her appeal to millions of followers.

JENNA MARBLES

The Jenna Marbles success story might be characterized by these five words: "I did it my way."

With over 13 million subscribers and over a billion total views, Jenna Mourey, a.k.a. Jenna Marbles, is without question YouTube's most popular female vlog personality — with a whopping emphasis on "personality."

A social media superstar who describes herself as a "comedian, YouTube entertainer, mother of two dogs, majestic internet creature, and unicorn," Marbles' pseudonym derives from the name of her chihuahua Charles Franklin Marbles, a.k.a Mr. Marbles, who often appears in videos with her alongside her other "furry child," an Italian greyhound named Kermit.

Born in Rochester, New York, Jenna did not bank on becoming a social media celeb, and unlike a lot of social media personalities, she did not initially aspire to a career in entertainment. She began making videos relatively late (2010), only after moving to Boston following high school, attaining a bachelor's degree in psychology from Suffolk University, and then going on to get a master's degree in sports psychology and counseling from Boston University.

Following graduate school, she stayed in Cambridge where, according to her blog, she "worked a bunch of random jobs for a while, none of which required being an actual grown up" while her new degree gathered dust. These jobs included bartending, blogging and working at a tanning salon.

Eventually she got a job writing for StoolLaLa, the female counterpart of the popular men's lifestyle blog Barstool, where she honed blogging and comedy skills that would serve her well in days to come.

It was around this time that she posted her first YouTube videos, including the famous "How to trick people into thinking you're good looking," which has received a staggering 58 million views to date. The clip exhibits a DIY template and telegenic comedy style that has come to define the unique Jenna Marbles brand. The *New York Times* described the video this way:

"In a dim, white-paneled bedroom, Ms. Mourey sat before her computer and began: 'If you were born really ugly like me, have no fear. There's steps you can take to be good-looking. Kind of.'

In a mesmerizing kind of reverse burlesque, her naked face and pale blue eyes disappeared under a flurry of foundation, false eyelashes and frosted pink lipstick.... 'There is no cure for ugly,' she says in her flat Rochester accent, 'but you can make yourself into a human optical illusion.'"

JENNA

Jenna Marbles throws out
the ceremonial first pitch
at Dodger Stadium in 2013.

Mourey enjoyed vlogging, and she discovered others in the online community who also made humorous videos. She cites among her early influences vloggers including *iJustine*, *Smosh*, Kingsley, Ryan Higa, Ray William Johnson and GloZell Green.

She continued to make videos and build an audience, and, after a year of saving money, she moved to Los Angeles to be closer to the YouTube community there. Jenna's DIY brand of comedy, dog-lover antics and social commentary hasn't changed substantially since her early days.

While many digital entertainers step up their technical game with more expensive lighting and higher production values as their popularity grows, Jenna's aesthetic remains reliably low-tech. She focuses instead on the comedy and content of her work, and is a savvy editor of her own videos, which she often conceives, shoots, edits and uploads in a single day.

Several vloggers have appeared on reality television, but the Jenna Marbles brand of humor has less in common with *The Real World*. She is more akin to Tina Fey and the comedy satire of *Saturday Night Live* and *South Park*. Her humor is consistently original and well-timed, the writing tight, and her material generally more inspired than most reality TV.

Mourey does quite well without any help from traditional media outlets. She has already turned down numerous offers. By doing it her way, Jenna has become the type of celebrity for which she seems particularly well-suited. She is a millionaire many times over. Unlike her peers, she has stated that she feels no great pressure to make the jump to TV or film.

"I'm not completely sold that you ever have to transition to mainstream media, you know?" she told the *L.A. Times*. "What I get to do is have fun in my house, by myself, and put it on the internet."

Operating as a one-woman studio, she produces a product that draws more than a million views every day — far more than many TV shows. She retains total creative freedom, shooting what she can handle alone in her house with only the help of her dogs. She uses her Facebook, Twitter, Instagram and Tumblr to keep in touch with her audience and polls them for video suggestions, forging a direct connection that would be impossible within the boundaries of traditional media.

Presenters Larry King and Jenna Marbles onstage at the 3rd Annual Streamy Awards at Hollywood Palladium

Jenna told the webseries *What's Trending* that she believes social media has democratized entertainment. She speculates that anyone can be a successful YouTube personality, and says, "As long as you're electric and awesome and your*self*, you can do whatever you want on YouTube. Anyone can do this." Her advice to others who aspire to social media stardom: "You have to start. Just jump, just do it, just start, don't turn back...and just be you. People like getting to know you, that's the whole idea about it, they want to know you."

Jenna posted her 200th video early in 2014 and she thanked her audience of over 13.5 million subscribers for sharing the best four years of her life.

MICHELLE PHAN

At 26, Michelle Phan (pronounced "fawn," like the baby deer) is another of social media's big success stories.

Born in Boston to a Vietnamese-American family, her Vietnamese name, Tuyêt Băng, means "avalanche," a word that is appropriate for describing her snowballing success. Phan waitressed as a teen to help her struggling family make ends meet. She lived with her mother and two siblings in a single room with only one bed and didn't own a

MICHELLE

computer. Given her YouTube success, it is remarkable to think that she didn't have her own computer until she was 20 when she was given a free laptop by her college. Phan filmed her very first makeup tutorial on it and now she has emerged as the most successful beauty guru on the internet.

When she was young, her family migrated to the San Francisco Bay Area, where they moved frequently, once changing houses six times in a single year. In her "Draw My Life" video, Michelle reveals that she later found out this was due to her father's gambling addiction. As she describes, they moved so often because he frequently lost the rent money in poker games, causing them to be evicted.

Moving a lot also meant changing schools. She remembers always being the shy new girl, and would retreat into her imagination to cope with loneliness. She loved art, and used to draw superheroes and Disney princesses, an early enthusiasm that would later be echoed as she showed viewers how to make themselves up like Catwoman, Mulan, Belle, Princess Jasmine and Snow White.

The Phans subsequently moved to Tampa, Florida, and one night, after a large gambling loss, her father, with whom she had been very close, abandoned the family in shame and despair. Michelle would not see him again for 10 years.

(Michelle also recalls experiencing racism during her time in Tampa, where she was one of the few Asian-Americans at her school.)

Michelle's mother, who Michelle describes as "a strong woman," was left to raise Michelle and her older brother Steve with meager financial resources. Her mother entered a second

marriage, during which Michelle's younger sister Christine was born, although the marriage didn't last. (Michelle has referred only obliquely in interviews to her stepfather, a subject she is reluctant to discuss publicly.)

Michelle credits her love of the beauty industry to her mother, who worked in a nail salon where Michelle would go after school and scour beauty magazines for new beauty techniques. Once she began allowing Michelle to wear makeup, she also shared her own beauty tips with her. She described herself during this time in a *Wall Street Journal* video interview as "a sponge, absorbing all this information, all these facts."

After high school, college seemed out of reach with the family's financial condition; however, Michelle's mother used money scraped together by aunts and uncles that was intended to help pay rent and buy some furniture, and used it to pay for Michelle's first semester of art school. The school furnished Michelle with her first computer, which would prove a life-altering gift.

"I promised [my mother] I would find a way to take care of the family. I just never imagined it would be through YouTube," she wrote in a 2013 *Glamour* magazine article.

> **"BEAUTY IS SOMETHING UNIVERSAL FOR BOTH MEN AND WOMEN."**
> **—MICHELLE PHAN**

"The makeup tutorials were a fun hobby at first…. I was resourceful: I stocked up on lipsticks and liner from drugstore 75-cent sale bins. As my YouTube following grew, I was soon earning as much from advertising revenue as from waiting tables, so I quit my job. My boss thought I was crazy, which just made me more determined. In 2012, four years and 200 videos later, my channel was so successful that Google offered me $1 million to create 20 hours of content. It was an incredible opportunity: out of all the online beauty experts, they had picked me, the person who filmed in her bedroom!"

She also began making videos for Lancome, a division of L'Oreal, although when a representative for the company called later that year, she thought she was being fired. Instead, the cosmetic giant invited her to launch her own makeup line, which she describes as her real Cinderella moment.

"I called my mom, who was giving someone a pedicure. 'Today is the last day you're doing that,' I said. 'I don't want you to go to work tomorrow.' As I told her about the project, we sobbed together uncontrollably."

Michelle's line is called *EM by Michelle Phan* (the "EM" stands for "a reflection of ME" and is also the Vietnamese word for "little sister" or "sweetie"). She started her own multichannel YouTube network called FAWN (the For All Women Network). She also launched Generation Beauty, a conference aimed at the plugged-in generation. She and other beauty vloggers, including Bethany Mota, were on hand to teach women how to produce their own high-quality, potentially lucrative online beauty videos.

When asked by the *Wall Street Journal* what she believes attracts viewers willing to listen to what she has to say, she responded, "Beauty is something universal for both men and women, and I think it's also something that's really easy. It's an affordable luxury for women."

Regarding her sensibility, she told *Forbes* (which listed Phan, along with Justin Bieber, in its roster of "Top Careers Launched Via YouTube"), "My production style is all about imagination. I want my audience to use their imagination when they watch my videos. My goal is for my voice to be that little hope of encouragement in your head when you walk out your door."

As she told the *WSJ,* "I like to inspire women to find their inner beauty, and makeup is an amazing tool to bring that inner beauty out."

In her *Glamour* article, she concluded with the following about her past, present and future: "... Even though makeup can change the way you look, I want everyone watching my videos to know perfection doesn't exist. ...My life hasn't been perfect, and look where I am today. I don't know what the future holds,

but I love working in the digital world. I never get bored; I went swimming in a mermaid tail for one of my last videos, which got 1.475 million views. Whatever happens, I'll just keep moving forward. Like an avalanche."

ZOE SUGG

Zoe Sugg is the 24-year-old fashion maven dominating the YouTube style scene on the other side of the Atlantic, via her wildly popular YouTube channel Zoella.

Zoe was born in Brighton, England on March 28, 1990, followed eighteen months later by brother Joe Sugg (YouTube's *ThatcherJoe*). She grew up in the idyllic rural village of Lacock in the county of Wiltshire, known for its unspoiled country appearance. (The village was featured briefly in two of the Harry Potter films, *Harry Potter and the Sorcerer's Stone*, in which Zoe was cast as an extra, and *Harry Potter and the Half-Blood Prince*.)

Zoe has been dating fellow YouTuber Alfie Deyes (*PointlessBlog*) for several years, and the couple are an active part of Britain's thriving YouTube social scene. This group includes Zoe's brother, Caspar Lee, and Marcus Butler, who collaborated with Zoe on the video

ZOE

"Accent Challenge," which won Best Challenge Video in Sugarscape's 2013 YouTuber Awards. Zoella was also voted Best Fashion & Beauty channel, and "Zalfie" were voted Cutest YouTube Couple.

Zoe has been filming and editing personal video documents from a very young age. "Vlogging At Age 11" depicts an 11-year old Zoe, already a personable and telegenic master of the medium, recording a video journal of herself loading her suitcase in preparation of a family holiday to Portugal. This predicted her future haul vlogs as she shows the camcorder each item of clothing, every pair of shoes and each accessory as she packs and provides a running commentary.

She began her official fashion and beauty vlog in February 2009, originally called zoella280390, incorporating her birthday in the moniker. This was expanded later the same year into a YouTube channel called simply Zoella, where she continued to focus on lifestyle and fashion topics, while also touching on issues of social anxiety, self-esteem and cyberbullying.

Zoe states in her "Draw My Life" video that she has struggled with social anxiety for years, which proved a problem for her after secondary school when many of her friends left for university. This was a difficult period for Zoe, as she felt alienated and like she had no direction. She worked unhappily in retail and interior design, but it was YouTube that eventually provided a way forward.

In 2010, she made contact with Louise Watson, a fellow YouTuber from Northampton who had her own style vlog called SprinkleOfGlitter. The two became best friends and have since made many collab videos together. They talk every day and travel the globe together attending YouTube functions and gatherings.

Zoella has amassed over 5.5 million YouTube subscribers and currently gets more than 12 million views each month. She has 1.6 million Twitter followers and two million Instagram followers. In June 2014, Penguin announced that it had signed a publishing deal with Zoella to pen two forthcoming novels; American and Canadian rights to the books were sold within 24 hours to Atria Books.

Her publisher describes her first novel *Girl Online* as a "modern day *Notting Hill* for teens" in which "an ordinary 15-year-old girl's relationship with an American pop star goes viral as her anonymous blog is exposed to the world." @

SPECIAL TRIBUTE TO ESTHER EARL

Although she was only 16 when she died following a four-year battle with thyroid cancer, Esther Grace Earl continues to inspire. After meeting writer John Green, an online hero of Esther's, at a Harry Potter fan conference in 2009, Esther became one of the inspirations for Hazel Grace Lancaster, the main character in his bestselling novel *The Fault in Our Stars* and its blockbuster film adaptation.

Esther was a candid and prolific writer in her own right. She shared her real-life narrative through social media platforms like Twitter, Formspring, Tumblr (as crazycrayon), on her YouTube channel cookie4monster4, and through the book *This Star Won't Go Out: The Life and Work of Esther Grace Earl*, a posthumously-published collection of Esther's journal writings and drawings, for which Green wrote the preface.

Esther was an enthusiastic member of the Nerdfighter community, and an activist in the Harry Potter Alliance, taking part in major efforts to raise money for human rights, literacy and disaster relief. In 2010, the HPA competed against 10,000 other charitable organizations to win a grant from Chase Community Giving on Facebook. Andrew Slack, the organization's cofounder, credits Esther for inspiring 38,689 people who voted online because of Esther and winning the first place grant of $250,000. The money was used to fund the HPA's literacy and LGBT

rights programs. The accomplishment drew the attention of author J.K. Rowling, who sent a hand-drawn picture of a magical Sorting Hat with the note: "To Esther, with love and best wishes always — Jo."

Confined and tethered by tubes for long periods while undergoing surgery and radio-iodine treatments, Esther reached out from her hospital bed to an ever-growing circle of friends. She maintained an active social media presence throughout her hospitalization. Esther was writing and vlogging constantly (in addition to her own vlog, she helped run the blog effyeahnerdfighters), doing collab videos, and staying in touch with a wide network of people who remember her unflagging optimism and humor.

Shortly before she passed away, Esther was granted a wish from the Make-A-Wish Foundation. They flew John Green and many of her friends to visit her in Boston. During the visit, John promised Esther that he and his brother Hank would make a video about whatever she wanted for their Vlogbrothers channel every year on August 9 — her birthday — which Green christened "Esther Day." Esther took a couple weeks to think about what she wanted, then delivered her answer.

Esther Day is dedicated, as per Esther's wish, to celebrating love among friends and family — a kind of love, Green submits, that is too often overlooked in our culture. We tend to stress romantic love in all of our media, for which there is already a holiday. "I think of Esther Day as a kind of Valentine's Day for all the other kinds of love," says Green. Esther Day is considered the most important holiday in Nerdighteria, the online community that follows the Vlogbrothers, John and Hank Green. Every year these Nerdfighters challenge people to say "I love you" to a beloved friend or family member, especially when it is difficult to do so.

The Harry Potter Alliance website, which suggests an annual Esther Day Project, said this: "Love is important. Love is what saved the wizarding world and, long before that, its residents. Fandoms become communities when we celebrate loving not just a book or a movie, but each other." Every year, friends, family and fans of Esther celebrate the day by making their own videos to remember her energy and life.

"She would have said herself that she lived a very full life," said her father, Wayne. "She didn't waste any time, she had a sense of what was important." After her death, Esther's parents founded "This Star Won't Go Out," a non-profit foundation which helps families who have children with cancer by providing funds to help pay for travel, rent and other expenses. The organization's website describes the motivation behind its mission: "A gift of money is really a gift towards quality time as a family — and that's a gift that is beyond value."

Esther is missed by those who knew her — she touched the lives of many during her brief but vibrant lifetime — but audiences continue to be captivated by her tale of tenacious spirit and courage. Her legacy and memory now also lives on in the hearts and minds of the millions of new fans who came to know and love her story. ★

CHAPTER FOUR

SEARCH FRIEND-GINE: GROUP THERAPY

HANNAH AND HILLY HINDI

Its interactive nature makes social media fertile ground for collaboration, and nearly every social media star participates in frequent collab projects. Most organizations that give online awards have special categories for collab vids, and there have been many creative collaborations since the inception of social media designed to entertain, inform and raise money for worthy causes.

You might recognize the names of several popular online collabs like *Smosh*, *O2L*, the *Janoskians*, the *Vlogbrothers*, the *Fine Brothers*, *Vsauce*, Jack Howard and Dean Dobbs (*Jack and Dean*), Rhett McLaughlin and Link Neal (*Rhett & Link*), Vine stars Jack Gallinsky and Jack Johnson (*Jack and Jack*), boyfriend-girlfriend duo *PrankvsPrank*, and dance parody sisters Hannah and Hilly Hindi (*The Hillywood Show*).

Online music collabs include girl groups Fifth Harmony and Cimorelli, Australian pop rockers 5 Seconds of Summer (5SOS), boybands Midnight Red, Before You Exit, Action Item and Forever In Your Mind, and country-singing sister act Megan & Liz.

The channel AwesomenessTV could be considered a sprawling collaboration that features a revolving cast of many of the most popular social media celebs doing their thing online as well as on Nickelodeon.

Here's a closer look at a few collabs that are making their mark in social media.

OUR2NDLIFE — Marketed as the "first vlogger supergroup," O2L is comprised of JC Caylen, Trevor Moran, Kian Lawley, Ricky Dillon, Sam Potorff and, until recently, Connor Franta. The channel has risen to become YouTube's biggest collab effort, with over 1.8 million subscribers. Collectively, the members' subscriber base tops 8 million.

Formed in 2012, O2L is essentially a continuing vlog-series made up of videos posted to YouTube by the six O2L members, individually and together, backed by multi-channel network Fullscreen. The group originally featured a seventh member, Ricardo Ordieres, who later left the channel to pursue a career in radio in April 2013.

Every week, the guys pick a different theme, and each member posts a new video to their collab channel on a different day: Tuesdays belong to Ricky Dillon, 21; Sam Pottorff, 17, takes the stage on Wednesdays; Thursdays are all about JC Caylen, 21; Fridays are the domain of Trevor Moran, the youngest of the bunch at 15; and Saturdays put Kian Lawley, 18, front and center. (Mondays used to be Connor Franta's "Frantastic Monday." He has not yet been replaced.)

The guys decided to form the O2L collaboration after rooming together at VidCon 2012. Online enthusiasm for the newly formed group, particularly among young female followers, flourished at a dizzying rate. By 2013, they had launched their own 20-city North American headline tour. $75 VIP tickets sold out at all venues in less than 30 minutes, and O2L was one of the biggest attractions on the first DigiTour, drawing thousands of screaming millennial fans across the U.S. and Canada.

Of the five members, only Moran and Dillon have any real performing credentials — Moran was a contestant on *The X-Factor*, and both have done music videos in which the non-singing members of the group make gratuitous appearances — but fans respond wildly to the mashup of simple dance moves, Q&As and YouTube-style live challenges that comprise O2L's live performances.

On tour they were accompanied by a documentary crew lead by Michael Goldfine, who produced *Camp*

Trevor Moran (c) and Our2ndLife on location during Moran's music video shoot in 2013.

Takota, a movie featuring YouTube stars Grace Helbig, Mamrie Hart and Hannah Hart. Goldfine filmed footage for a planned feature film documenting O2L's burgeoning popularity and the insurgent rise of the social media star phenomenon.

"We saw O2L's potential when Sam, Kian and JC initially appeared at DigiFest NYC 2012," said Meridith Viliando Rojas, co-founder and CEO of the Ryan Seacrest-backed DigiTour Media, speaking to the British-American social media website *Mashable*. "They are the ideal act to take on the road because of their huge community of engaged fans. We look forward to working with Fullscreen on the documentary."

Brimming with marketing potential, the members have signed brand endorsements left and right: Invisalign (sponsor of DigiTour), Nokia, AT&T, Hulu, AXE, Coca-Cola, to name a few. In April, MTV enlisted the group, along with other YouTubers such as Bethany Mota, Rebecca Black, Tyler Oakley, Jenn McAllister and Andrea Russett, to create promos and act as social media correspondents for the MTV Movie Awards, taking over MTV's Twitter feed for the evening to interview nominees and post Tweets from the red carpet.

THE VLOGBROTHERS — In 2007, the Green brothers, John, 36, and Hank, 33, began a YouTube project they called *Brotherhood 2.0*, which was intended as a way to stay in touch with each other by a less impersonal method than phone texting. The series of weekly vlogs between the brothers has evolved into one of the most far-reaching and influential collaborations in all of social media.

John Michael Green is a vlogger, entrepreneur and best-selling, award-winning young adult author whose latest novel, *The Fault in Our Stars*, debuted at number one on the *New York Times* Best Seller list in 2012. In 2014, the film adaptation of the same name opened at number one at the box office. John was referred to as a "teen whisperer" and a "prophet in a universal, all-things-connected sort of context" in a profile written by actress Shailene Woodley for *Time* magazine's list of the 100 Most Influential People of 2014. (Woodley portrays a character inspired by Green's friend and fellow YouTuber Esther Earl in the motion picture version of *The Fault in Our Stars*.)

William Henry "Hank" Green, III, is an entrepreneur, biochemist, musician and vlogger. In addition to his Vlogbrothers pursuits, he is the creator of the environmental technology blog EcoGeek, and the developer of Subbable, an online crowdfunding platform that allows audiences to support projects of their choice by subscribing to them and making monthly financial contributions.

Of the many proponents and practitioners of social media, the Green brothers seem to understand its power, appeal and potential (as well as its growing pains) better than anyone. Of YouTube's emerging place on the media landscape, John Green has this to say:

"One of my favorite things about YouTube is that there's no bright line between creators and viewers. There's no firm, fast distinction between people

> **THE VLOGBROTHER MOTTO IS MEANT TO REMIND PEOPLE TO CELEBRATE WHAT IS POSITIVE AND UNIQUE ABOUT THEMSELVES AND TO DO THEIR BEST.**

who make stuff and people who watch stuff, because most of the creators are viewers, and most of the viewers are also creators, whether they're creating their own videos or their own comments or whatever. They are creating."

The Greens' capacity to shape their own vision, as well as their support of the creative endeavors of others, is huge. Their mix of brainy, fast-talking info-tainment, tongue-in-cheek humor and social awareness serve as the vehicle by which the brothers spread their message across the globe, summed up by their central motto: DFTBA (Don't Forget To Be Awesome).

The Vlogbrother motto is meant to remind people to celebrate what is positive and unique about themselves and to do their best. By reminding people not to forget to be awesome, their stated aim is to help Decrease World Suck (another motto). In Vlogbrother lingo, this means trying to help make the world a better place.

John and Hank number among their primary influences vlog pioneer Ze Frank, who they cite as "the original video blogger, our hero." (Frank, considered one of the most influential people in the field, is now the executive vice president of video at BuzzFeed, producing original

William Henry "Hank" Green, III, is an entrepreneur, biochemist, musician and vlogger.

programming for the social news and entertainment site.)

Since its modest beginnings, the Vlogbrothers brand has evolved in far-reaching directions. Aside from their main channel, the Greens also launched the channel Crash Course, which focuses on education and was initially funded by YouTube's $100 million Original Channel Initiative. This was shortly followed by *SciShow*, a series of science-related videos hosted by Hank, and a number of other education-related projects. SciShow Space, a new channel devoted to space related science, news and discoveries, is also hosted by Hank Green.

With seemingly tireless energy, the brothers have embarked on a number of other enterprises that spool out from the central hub of their massive online base. These include a gaming channel (hankgames), a quiz show called Truth or Fail, a record label which releases material by a number of YouTubers and other artists (DFTBA Records), and an array of Nerdfighter merchandising. They are also responsible for jointly co-founding Subabble, which began as a way to underwrite the continued production of *Crash Course*, and now supports the financing of various other web series.

The Vlogbrothers encourage their subscribers [see Nerdfighteria] to branch out and participate in projects such

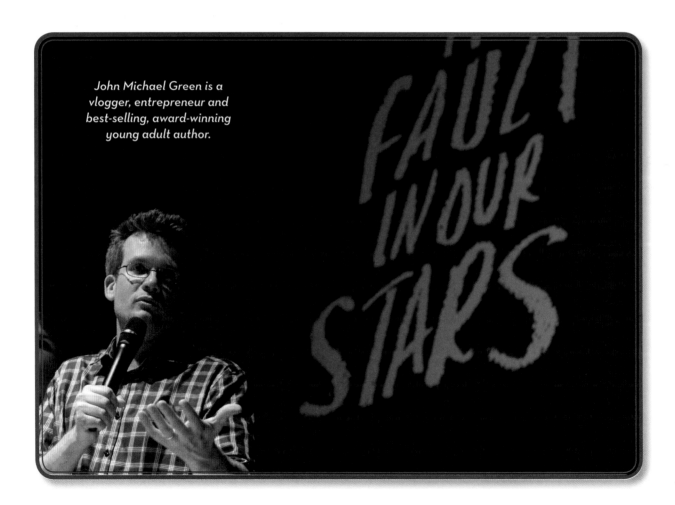

John Michael Green is a vlogger, entrepreneur and best-selling, award-winning young adult author.

as their subscriber-driven charitable effort Project 4 Awesome (P4A), which has held annual charitable events every December since 2007. P4A urges people to reach out via social media to promote their favorite charities, using their personal social network to raise charitable awareness over a two-day period and raise money for their charitable cause of choice. P4A raised over a quarter of a million dollars for charity in 2013.

They are also, of course, the founders and organizers of the enormously successful VidCon, which has grown into the largest convention of its kind in the world [see DigiFest, Vidcon & More].

Talk of the Green brothers leads naturally to their sprawling fanbase, which might be seen as a sort of collaboration unto itself: Nerdfighteria.

NERDFIGHTERIA — While more of a hydra-like entity than one specific online collaboration, the Vlogbrothers' highly motivated and mobilized social movement nevertheless merits special mention. Nerdfighters, collectively known as Nerdfighteria, began as a fanbase for John and Hank Green's Vlogbrothers channel, although it soon morphed into an internet subculture, gaining momentum and embracing a remarkable degree of real world activism.

Nerdfighteria has made grassroots efforts in areas of local community building, organized Christmas concerts and gift exchanges, and have launched fundraising campaigns and charity drives aimed at various social causes. Nerdfighter parlance emphasizes that "personal awesomeness" has a ripple effect that helps build an awesome community, a concept perhaps best exemplified in the movement's Project 4 Awesome charitable achievements. In the words of one Nerdfighter: "You're not awesome just for yourself. You're awesome for the people around you."

The sprawling Nerdfighter network now encompasses an official forum, numerous chat rooms, a Reddit board and a dedicated Minecraft server. Thousands of Nerdfighter meetup groups are searchable via the Nerdfighters Directory (http://effyeahnerdfighters. com/localnfgroups), which lists resources on seven continents and in every U.S. state. A nine-page list of hundreds of Nerdfighter projects can be found at http://nerdfighters.ning.com/page/ nerdfighter-projects. There is even an unofficial Nerdfighter holiday: Esther Day, established in 2007 and named in honor of Esther Earl [see special section "A Tribute To Esther Earl"].

In 2010, one of four airplanes headed for Haiti filled with food, supplies and medicine bought with proceeds from Nerdfighter charity efforts was christened the SS DFTBA. (The other three planes were named for Harry Potter characters.)

There is also a subgroup of Nerdfighters called Kiva who loan money to entrepreneurs in the developing world. They use a model similar to Kickstarter, through which members can allot money that is then made available to fund loans to people all over the world. $4,198,375 has been issued in loans through Kiva in areas such Agriculture, Energy, Textiles, Retail, Restaurants and Higher Education.

In a moment of international Nerdfighter visibility and solidarity, British gymnast Jennifer Pinches flashed the Nerdfighters hand sign for the cameras (yes, there is a hand sign — an adaptation of the Vulcan "Live Long and Prosper" salute, done with both hands, arms crossed, palms facing inward) following her routine in the all-round women's team finals at the 2012 Summer Olympics in London. *Star Trek* and *Sherlock* star Benedict Cumberbatch and *Doctor Who*'s Matt Smith have also been seen displaying the Nerdfighter "gang sign."

The subject of Nerdfighteria occupies almost two full episodes of Benjamin Cook's "Becoming YouTube," an intelligent web series profiling YouTubers in the UK, many of whom are associated with the Nerdfighter movement. The fourth episode, titled "What Is A Nerdfighter (And So Can You)," explores some aspects of Nerdfighteria. He includes scattered criticism in regard to some individual Nerdfighters' behavior being interpreted as elitist and exclusionary to those who

THE NERDFIGHTER HAND SIGN USES BOTH HANDS, ARMS CROSSED, AND PALMS FACING INWARD.

don't identify as Nerdfighters, especially in particular areas of fan culture. A few noted YouTubers express frustration with some Nerdfighters' tendency to stray from the positive message at the heart of the movement. They tend to get lost in a kind of one-upmanship with regard to things that Nerdfighters are supposed to like, such as video games, Harry Potter, Doctor Who and John Green's books.

In the next episode, titled "A Conversation With John Green," John himself addresses this point. He suggests that a growing community always has the potential to be somewhat messy. However, he believes that superficial shared interests aren't nearly as important as a values-based identity, and how you imagine the world around you is what defines being a Nerdfighter. Green also stresses the value of keeping social media in perspective relative to real life.

"I think that there is great joy and fulfillment to be found in real life relationships between physical human beings, and I don't think the internet is an effective replacement for those things, and I don't think it's supposed to be. To me, it's just a different way of being with people, and a different way of talking

AUTHOR JOHN GREEN STRESSES THE VALUE OF KEEPING SOCIAL MEDIA IN PERSPECTIVE RELATIVE TO REAL LIFE.

about stuff that matters with people who matter to you. I don't buy the argument that, 'I don't need a life because I have the internet.'"

Millions of teens around the world have found in Nerdfighteria a movement that incites them to strive and excel, online and in real life, with its central message: DFTBA.

JACKSGAP — One of the most popular collabs on the web is made up of identical twins Jackson Frayn Harries and Finnegan Frayn Harries, better known as Jack and Finn, and known collectively by their YouTube channel name Jacksgap.

The Finn brothers' good looks and gentlemanly behavior attract a lot of female viewers, with 88% of their 3.4 million subscribers falling into this demographic. Rabid fan-girls bombard them with mountains of heart-covered mail, camp out in front of their residence, and mob airports to see them.

For girls who don't already know these things (and for everyone else), Jack and Finn's Tumblr lists the following details about them: They were born on May 13, 1994. Finn is the elder twin, by two minutes. Jack is a full-time professional YouTuber, and he acted in the TV show *School of Comedy*. Finn is a graphic designer (he designed the Jacksgap logo and is responsible for the channel's branding) and a filmmaker. They have a dog named Toto, and Jack used to have a bearded lizard named Sidney that Finn was afraid of (Jack had to give Sid up for adoption when he left for university, and now has a pair of tiny tortoises named Herbert and Doris). Both boys attended the exclusive Harrodian School (actors Robert Pattinson and Tom Sturridge also studied there). Finn took Spanish; Jack took French. They have a sister named Emmy Lou.

The Harries brothers were born in London, and are the product of multiple generations of highly accomplished, media-savvy writers. Their father is Andy Harries, an extremely successful British television producer and former journalist; their mother is filmmaker and novelist Rebecca Frayn. They are the maternal grandsons of eminent playwright Michael Frayn and noted biographer Claire Tomalin.

Originally launched by Jack on June 12, 2011, to document his college gap year (the year off before he started college), Jacksgap began as a solo effort. However, his brother Finn's appearance in his videos marked a dramatic spike in the channel's viewership, so the siblings decided to make it a joint venture. They started posting videos together over the next three years and their subscribed base has skyrocketed to over 3 million. The channel has its own short theme song, sung by Jack, comprised of the lyrics, "Jack's Gap, Jack's Gap, five minutes of your life that you won't get back."

In a 2012 article in the *Telegraph*, Finn said, "What's great about YouTube is that we have total control over the content. Instead of having a £6,000 professionally built website, we do it ourselves — for free. Nobody is telling us what to do or when to post; we don't have to ask the adults to help us anymore. I guess in

JACKSGAP

our parents' day, kids used to listen to rock-and-roll music in their bedrooms as a form of rebellion. This is our little rebellion. YouTube is our world."

The twins use their bedrooms as offices, employing iPads, cameras, lights and multiple computer screens for shooting and editing footage (both are self-taught). Their videos are scripted in advance — they spend up to two hours a

day on YouTube, researching the latest trends — and it can take up to three days to film them.

"It's a full-time job," Jack told the *Telegraph*. "We don't have a lot of time to do other things. You're putting your personal life out there on the web, so every day you're working, whether you want to or not. I'll tweet or take a photograph every time I'm out; you never switch off."

By 2012, the ad revenue from their YouTube channel provided enough funds for the twins to embark on a trip to Thailand, which they duly documented for their viewers. They treated fans to a video of Jack doing a naked bungee jump in celebration of reaching 100,000 subscribers (the video has since drawn over 3 million views).

In 2013, they branched out from their 5-minute format, using £20,000 from Skype, Sony and MyDestination to fund a series of four 15-minute episodes about their travels in India. They spent three weeks there with friends, participating in an event called the Rickshaw Run, which organizes treks across India to raise money for charitable causes. Their team included fellow social media stars Jake Foushee (the teen voiceover artist from North Carolina known for his vocal impressions on YouTube and Vine) and English food-stunt/travel vlogger Louis Cole (viewers can see him eat live cockroaches and scorpions on his channel *FoodForLouis*, and follow his adventures on the road on *FunForLouis*). The group toured 3,500 kilometers across the width of the country, from Kochi to Shillong, in motorized rickshaws while raising £177,521 (over $250,000 USD) for the Teenage Cancer Trust, far exceeding their goal of £100,000.

In May 2014, their channel won the Screenchart! Channel Award for Best Directing, and "The Rickshaw Run" took the award for Best Mini-Series or Short Film.

The brothers continue to make videos, are active members of the UK social media crowd, and take part in numerous charity efforts on which many of their current YouTube videos are based.

THE JANOSKIANS — The Aussie group — whose acronymic moniker stands for Just Another Name of Silly Kids in Another Nation — is comprised of brothers Beau Brooks, 21, Jai Brooks, 19, and Luke Brooks, 19 (Jai and Luke are twins); plus Daniel "Skip" Sahyounie, 19,

and James Yammouni, 18, all of whom have been friends since their grammar school days in Melbourne.

The Janoskians began posting videos on YouTube in 2011. On TwinTalkTime, brothers Jai and Luke share observations about being twins. They also have their own AwesomenessTV channel, on which they bring teen audiences more of the Janoskians brand of rowdy prank humor.

In 2012, they were picked up by Sony Records Australia, and have produced four music singles to date. Their first single, "Set the World On Fire," was co-written by Beau Brooks and first released on their YouTube channel. It went on to reach number 19 on the Australian charts. It was followed by "Best Friends" and a world tour in 2013, and this year has seen the release of two more video-supported singles, "This Freakin Song" and "Real Girls Eat Cake," which they will perform on their second world tour, called the Got Cake Tour.

A clip of one of their stunts was featured on *The Ellen Degeneres Show*, in which they sneak up on unsuspecting mall shoppers and try to dance behind their backs without them noticing. In 2012, they produced an eight-episode web series for MTV Australia called *The Janoskians: MTV Sessions*, which

JANOSKIANS

aired on MTV Australia's website and showcased the boys pulling pranks on the public and each other.

In January 2014, streetwear apparel company the Putnam Accessory Group announced the launch of a Janoskians-designed clothing line called Dirty Pig. The label will include tees, beanies, snapbacks and sweatshirts featuring its brand logo — a picture of a winking pink pig — designed by Jai Brooks.

Jai Brooks was romantically linked with pop singer Ariana Grande in 2013, during which time online gossip about

the couple abounded. Their frequent breakups and reunions played out on Twitter and in the press, with Jai publicly accusing Grande of cheating on him with boy band member Nathan Sykes, which Grande refuted in interviews, calling Brooks' online rant "hurtful and shocking." By December 2013, reports noted that the pair had broken up, only to get back together again in May 2014, when they were seen together at the iHeart Radio awards. By the Teen Choice Awards in August 2014, they were rumored to have split for good and Grande was seen hand in hand with rapper Big Sean.

In 2013, the Janoskians embarked on their #NotABoyBand world tour, which sold out its entire run. They have since spread their brand to include an iTunes/Android video game app called Ouch!Couch, and signed a record deal with Republic Records in March 2014. Personal appearances in Los Angeles, New York, Melbourne and London resulted in closed-down venues due to teeming crowds of fans who turned out to get a glimpse of them. In May, Lionsgate announced that they will try to turn the Janoskians' internet following into box-office gold in a forthcoming feature film.

The members individually have more than 1 million followers each on Twitter, and their YouTube channels continue to draw big numbers. Their latest single "Real Girls Eat Cake" has garnered more than 4.7 million views, and they have 1.7 million subscribers on their AwesomenessTV channel. @

TOUR DE FORCE: DIGIFEST, VIDCON & MORE

Real time gatherings have sprung up everywhere in the wake of social media's outgrowth. These range from small, informal campus clubs to annual industry events like **Playlist Live** and **VidCon** held in sold-out convention centers. There are also more recent phenomena like **DigiFest** and **INTOUR**, festival gatherings aimed specifically at the fans of social media's newest stars.

DigiTour Media, the company behind **DigiFest** and the **DigiTour**, was founded in 2010 by Meredith Viliando Rojas, a former A&R rep for Columbia Records, and multi-platinum producer Christopher Rojas. Festival backers include *American Idol* host Ryan Seacrest and Advance Publications, parent company of Conde Nast. According to CEO Meredith Rojas, the tour presents the "creme de la meme" and the best of what's trending in social media.

The first DigiTour, which took place in 2011, was sponsored by YouTube and began with a multi-camera livestream at Google Headquarters in Mountainview, California, before embarking on a tour of 27 North American cities. Appearances were made by the Gregory Brothers, MysteryGuitarMan, David Choi and DeStorm. On opening night at the El Rey Theater in Los Angeles, papparazzi spotted pop star Britney Spears slipping out of the venue with her head concealed beneath a blanket after clandestinely checking out the event.

The first official DigiFest took place June 1, 2013 at New York's 3000-seat Terminal 5. General admission tickets went for $35 for the seven-hour all-ages event, which featured Joey Graceffa, Pentonix, Caspar Lee and Ahmir. For hardcore fans who could afford to splurge, 200 $99 VIP tickets were available. This ticket bought exclusive access to the rooftop VIP Artist Lounge, a numbered limited edition poster and a laminate pass, plus entrance to the venue one hour before doors opened to the public.

For those unable to make the trip to New York, the Terminal 5 event kicked off DigiTour 2013. The show hit the road for the rest of the year, traveling the U.S. and Canada with a roster that included popular British personalities such as Zoella, Marcus Butler, Alfie Deyes and Tanya Burr, collectively known as The Brit Crew.

In 2014, **DigiFest NYC** was held in the parking lot of CitiField in Queens. It drew 12,500 fans — almost as big a crowd as some of the New York Mets games that are held inside CitiField — and featured more than 85 performances, many of them under 15 minutes long. The lineup included stars of YouTube, Vine and Instagram such as Tyler Oakley, Connor Franta, Cody Johns, Trevor Moran, Troye Sivan, Caspar Lee, Kingsley, Fifth Harmony, the Janoskians, Jake Foushee, Nash Grier, Jenn McAllister and Andrea Russett.

The event featured gaming booths, beauty booths, music performances, sketch comedy and live Q&As. The onstage appearances were accompanied by prolonged bouts of screaming from fans. ("We had to build five to 10 minutes into the start of the show where we just let them scream and scream," Connor Franta told the *New York Times*.)

"These social media tastemakers are the rock stars of today and tomorrow," Rojas has suggested. "They influence so many people with their videos and unrivaled ability to empower fans who follow their every move. Their channels average millions of views and their daily videos on their second channels get watched 250,000-500,000 times each day — more than most TV news programs. The engagement these personalities have is unprecedented."

DigiTour UK extended the festival's reach to a British audience, bringing the whole gang to the famous Hammersmith Apollo in London. The show was streamed live online and was headlined by *X-Factor* contestants Union J.

Since its inception, DigiTour has sold over a quarter of a million tickets, and expects to double that number in 2015, with continuing events scheduled across the country.

If Digifest is social media's equivalent of SXSW, VidCon is online video's Lollapalooza.

Founded by social media titans John and Hank Green, **VidCon** is a convention dedicated specifically to the video-making aspect of social media. It has grown to be the largest convention of its kind in the world, attracting both creators and fans of online content as well as entertainment industry representatives from all areas of traditional media.

Internet personality Grace Helbig attends VidCon at Anaheim Convention Center on June 27, 2014 in Anaheim, California

According to their enrollment site, VidCon "is both an industry conference and a great big party." The Green brothers have expressed their mission statement as follows: "We want people to make important business contacts to grow their companies and careers, but we would prefer that they do it while dancing to a rock song about Doctor Who."

The first VidCon was a sold-out three-day event held at the Hyatt Regency Century Plaza hotel in Los Angeles. It drew 1,400 people and featured daytime panels and presentations by video makers and industry leaders, as well as nightly concerts featuring musicians who had achieved success mainly by presenting their music through the medium of online video. Subsequent years have seen VidCon explode to nearly 10 times its original size, eventually moving to the much larger Anaheim Convention Center and selling out up to two months in advance, with attendance swelling to over 18,000. Social media figures present have included Connor Franta, Toby Turner, Smosh, iJustine, PrankvsPrank, Joey Graceffa, Alfie Deyes, Grace Helbig, Joe Sugg, Troye Sivan, Caspar Lee, Tanya Burr, Corey Vidal and many, many more.

There are more social media fests springing up all over the world, including **SocialCon** in Chicago — a convention-style gathering running in conjunction with Chicago Comic-Con — and newcomer **InTour**, an in-person interactive social festival held in Pasadena, California in 2014. It was created by multi-channel online network Fullscreen, which teamed up with Warped Tour production company 4Fini to produce the event, and asked Marc Warzecha of Second City to direct it. InTour features Fullscreen's own roster of online talent, which has a significant overlap with DigiTour and VidCon, including Connor Franta, Ricky Dillon, Brent Rivera, *jennxpenn* and Alx James.

No matter where you live, you will soon be able to catch a gathering of your favorite social media stars at a venue near you. ★

CHAPTER FIVE

NEW KIDS ON THE BLOCK: INSTAGRAM, VINE AND SNAPCHAT

In the world of social media stardom, YouTube is the undisputed big man on campus. However, digital stars are also reaching an audience on platforms such as Pheed and Flickr, and especially on the short-format apps Instagram, Vine and Snapchat.

Initially a photo-sharing service, Instagram has seen its numbers grow exponentially to over 150 million active users. It began allowing users to post 15-second video clips in June 2013, and the use of hashtags make the content searchable.

KING BACH

For those with half the attention span, there is Vine. Owned by Twitter and launched in January 2013, Vine is the video sharing app that lets users film, edit, post, browse and view clips that are a mere six seconds long. It is sort of like a mini-YouTube, where viewers can find scores of micro-vids in the space of a few minutes. Vine's popularity has spread like wildfire, and Twitter estimates that five Tweets per second contain a Vine link.

Snapchat is the service that lets people upload posts which expire in 10 seconds, or use its Stories feature, which allows posts to have a 24-hour lifespan before they vanish. Most of Snapchat's estimated 90 million active users are between the age of 13 and 25. The clips may be brief, but a great deal of work can go into making short-format videos — some Viners work for hours filming, editing and scoring their material to produce a single six-second loop, and sometimes 100 takes are done to make one snippet of finished video.

A few mainstream stars such as Justin Bieber, Kim Kardashian, Beyoncé, Ariana Grande, Selena Gomez, Miley Cyrus and Josh Peck regularly post Instagram and Vine content that is followed by millions. Other names have emerged from obscurity to become bonafide short-format stars, entertaining viewers with strings of microvlogs, skits, stunts and comedy sketches compressed into six-second nutshells, attesting to what Shakespeare may have meant when he wrote that brevity is the soul of wit.

Social media fame has already led to mainstream recognition for **Andrew Bachelor, a.k.a King Bach**, who is one of Vine's biggest stars with over 8.1 million subscribers. Many of his six-second videos take a humorous poke at racial issues, and his comic timing has landed him a recurring role in Showtime's *House of Lies*. He has also found gigs in the main cast of MTV2's *Wild 'N Out* and on the Adult Swim series *Black Jesus*.

Brittany Furlan has been with Vine since the beginning, making her a true veteran of the still-relatively-new platform. With 7.2 million followers, she is the highest ranked female Viner and the third most subscribed Vine personality overall. The 2014 Daytime Emmy Awards, in a bid to attract a crossover audience, tapped Brittany to host their red carpet show along with Lauren Elizabeth, Meghan Rosette and Jessica Harlow. The controversial choice to use social media stars to provide TV coverage was widely considered a disaster, proving embarrassing for the show and the stars

> **SOME VINERS WORK FOR HOURS FILMING, EDITING AND SCORING THEIR MATERIAL TO PRODUCE A SINGLE SIX-SECOND LOOP.**

being interviewed, largely because the hosts seemed to know very little about daytime television. Their questions and comments were criticized as being ill-informed, "wildly unprofessional" and, in a few cases, offensive. Furlan admitted that she found the mismatch awkward and embarrassing. The L.A.-based humorist continues to hone her comedy skills online, still posting at least one clip per day after nearly two years on Vine, and she is currently at work on a female-driven sketch show, with actor and *Robot Chicken* creator Seth Green executive producing.

Frenchman **Jerome Jarre** is the fourth most followed individual on

Vine, and has been one of the defining presences on the app since its release. His video "Don't be afraid of love!" was one of Vine's early hits, and he has since amassed 7.1 million subscribers, plus 2.1 million followers on Shapchat. Tapping into the ever-expanding reach of short-form video and its marketing potential, Jarre co-founded the company **Grape Story**, which describes itself as "a mobile-first marketing agency and production house focused on pairing the best micro-content creators with innovative brands to tell powerful and engaging short stories."

Brothers **Marcus Johns** and **Cody Johns** are two more Vine veterans, and the West Palm Beach natives have built up massive followings with their comedy sketches, Hollywood good looks and a desire to tell stories within the medium's six-second format. Elder sibling Cody is a 24-year-old aspiring actor living in L.A., who was one of the very first people to join Vine. After gathering enough followers to attract sponsorship, the marketing potential of micro-video sharing became evident when the proceeds from a single Vine ad campaign that he worked on paid off his entire college tuition. Building on personal experience, Cody is currently

the creative director of Niche, a startup that connects brands with popular users on social media. He also continues to post videos on Vine, and currently has over 2.7 million subscribers.

Marcus, 20, was encouraged by his older brother to join Vine. Over time, he has become the more prolific Viner of the two, with over 5.2 million followers, consistently ranking him among the top Vine personalities. Marcus was selected by Fandango to be the company's social media correspondent for the 2014 Oscars. He took over Fandango's Instagram and YouTube accounts for the evening to post from the red carpet.

Rudy Mancuso is another top Vine celeb who plays on his own Brazilian and Italian heritage to skewer stereotypes and make people laugh. He has a repertoire of characters such as Spanish Batman and Spanish Superman, gaining him 5.5 million subscribers along the way.

Lele Pons is a 17-year-old Miami prep schooler who has photobombed her way to 4.2 million Vine followers. She became the very first Vine user ever to reach over a billion plays. In her clips, she often says, "Do it for the Vine" — and "doing it" includes giving a new bride and a cop pies in the face, spanking strangers on the street, and teaming up with a bevy of

YouTube and Vine personalities Nash Grier, Carter Reynolds, Matthew Espinosa, Cameron Dallas and Logan Paul at the 2014 Billboard Music Awards.

other Viners to perform humorous skits on topics such as embarrassing herself in front of boys and going clothes shopping with her dad.

Energetic 19-year-old Vine superstar **Logan Paul** became an Internet success practically overnight after he began posting humorous skits to the site in July 2013. The former high-school wrestler and all-star football player from Ohio has since collected over 5 million followers who regularly watch his combustive clips, which include one of him jumping over a fast-moving oncoming car (don't

try this at home!) and several of him staging impromptu wrestling matches in supermarkets. A YouTube compilation of his Vine work has had nearly 7 million views. Logan also distributes videos on

Snapchat, saying that the app's don't-blink-or-you'll-miss-it format adds a sense of urgency to the mix. In a February 2014 article, *Wired* magazine said this of Paul: "Just as the 140-character limit on

Twitter inspired new heights of succinct textual creativity, so too has the six-ish second limit of a Vine video produced a new type of snack-sized comedy. Paul has perfected the art of getting straight to the punchline." Since leaving Ohio to pursue a career in film and television and further his digital media ambitions, Logan's short videos have provided a springboard into longer-format entertainment. He now lives in West Hollywood with his brother **Jake Paul** (who often appears in Logan's videos and has over 2 million Vine followers of his own), and he recently scored a role in the Fox comedy series *Weird Loners*.

Also hugely popular on Vine are the boys (and one girl) originally associated with Magcon, a tour management group that has included top Viners and DigiTour heartthrobs **Nash Grier, Cameron Dallas, Matt Espinosa, Shawn Mendes, Taylor Caniff, Jacob Whitesides, Aaron Carpenter, Carter Reynolds, Hayes Greer,** and **Jack Gilinsky** and **Jack Johnson** of **Jack and Jack**. The crew's sole female member is Mahogany Gordy, who is the granddaughter of music industry legend Barry Gordy, and who goes by the online name **Mahogany LOX**. (Mahogany is also the sister of Skyler Gordy, half of "I'm Sexy and I Know It"

duo LMFAO, and Mahogany acted as DJ during the Magcon tour for the group's onstage appearances.)

Some of the Magcon bunch have used their fame constructively — for Shawn Mendes, Vine stardom was a launchpad toward a music career, helping him snag a deal with Island Records in January. His debut single "Life of the Party" debuted at number 24 on the Billboard Hot 100, making him, at 15, the youngest artist to debut in the top 25. The song also shot briefly to No. 1 on the iTunes download charts thanks in large part to mobilization of his large Twitter following. He is currently on tour with Austin

> **"[LOGAN] PAUL HAS PERFECTED THE ART OF GETTING STRAIGHT TO THE PUNCHLINE."**
> **—WIRED**

Nicholas Megalis at the 6ᵗʰ Annual Shorty Awards in 2014.

Vine duo *Jack and Jack*, have over 7.5 million followers combined across their Twitter, Vine and Instagram profiles. Their faces grace the side of the DigiTour bus. Like others before them, they hope to use their online following to boost a music career, and have recorded songs that include "Distance" and "Do It Right." *Jack and Jack* also headlined INTOUR, a new interactive festival featuring some of social media's top teen stars, including *jennxpenn*, Ricky Dillon and former *O2L* member Connor Franta.

Others who have made their mark on Instagram, Snapchat and Vine include **Alx James, Jerry Purpdrank, Shaun McBride, Chris Carmichael, Brent Rivera, Nicholas Megalis, Jack Baran (*ThatSoJack*), Bo Burnham, Landon Moss, Roberto Martin, Sunny Mabrey, Manon Matthews, Curtis Lepore, KC James, Jordan Burt, Eric Dunn, *DEM_WHITE_BOYZ*, Robby Alaya, Michael LoPriore, DeStorm, Chip Hock, Marlo Meekins, Simone Shepard, Thomas Sanders, Christian Del Grasso, Max Jr, Iman Crosson (*Alphacat*), Jessi Smiles, Tina Woods (*TooTurntTina*)** and **Lauren Giraldo (*Princess Lauren*)**. @

Mahone, and took home the award for Best Webstar in Music at the 2014 Teen Choice Awards.

Omaha natives Jack Gilinsky, 17, and Jack Johnson, 18, who comprise the

WHAT'S NEXT?

When The Fine Brothers asked a handful of teens in one of their Teens React videos if they considered Shane Dawson famous, one of the teens answered, "I consider him YouTube famous." When asked to define the difference between YouTube Famous and regular famous, she responded: "Well, regular famous is, you're kind of like a household name. But YouTube famous, your audience is kind of like, kids, so only some people know of you."

With YouTube raking in over a trillion total views, and given the growing potential for crossover promotion — Shane Dawson and Jenna Marbles have appeared on the cover of *Variety* since the comment above was made — it's clear that the line between social media-famous and regular-famous is becoming blurred. The day when social media-famous actually equates to household name-famous grows closer as online personalities cross over into mainstream awareness.

But does crossing over herald the end of what makes internet stars special to their fans?

In September, a front-page article in the *New York Times* noted the encroachment of Hollywood-style deal makers into the world of YouTube stardom. With top social media celebs now making well over $1 million a year, agents, managers, lawyers, producers and publicists have been swooping in to claim their piece of the pie. Startup companies have

formed for the express purpose of representing online talent, and established agencies are making aggressive moves to acquire internet stars for their roster. Mainstream networks and studios are also scrambling to tap into the fans of people like Bethany Mota and Shane Dawson.

As a result, internet stars once known for their accessibility and for cutting out the middle man are increasingly employing middle men of their own who have a say in what they produce, who they work with, who they talk to, who they see. Some social media stars appeared at DigiFest this year surrounded by teams of handlers and publicists who vetted their interactions with fans as well as brand reps and rival managers. Agents now comb social media gatherings, maneuvering behind the scenes and shaking hands, trying to get in with the new in-crowd.

As online stars adopt the tools and power structure of mainstream media, how will the current landscape of social media entertainment be altered? Do fans want to have to go through a screen of handlers to reach their favorite online personalities? Will fans looking for a direct personal experience be open to an environment that too closely mirrors the old-school Hollywood machine? Will they accept the sight of once-approachable online stars suddenly being cordoned off by velvet ropes, and hearing them say things like "Your people need to get in touch with my people"? And will they still be able to see the reflections they are looking for when windows of tinted glass roll up in their faces and a limo bears Shane Dawson away into a remote Hollywood sunset?

And for content creators, does the advent of deal makers and image strategists signal a sacrifice of honesty and authenticity? Will it render them less relatable to their audience? More sanitized? More distant? Less relevant?

Those questions are still being answered. Perhaps the Fine Brothers will make a clip titled "Teens React to Social Media Stars Who Go Mainstream."

When Jenna Marbles and Shane Dawson recently appeared in *Variety*, the article contrasted the pair's different attitudes toward crossing over. Dawson expressed an eagerness to enter mainstream television and film, while Marbles appeared less than willing to exploit the power of her 1.4 billion views, and remains reluctant to allow herself to be blinded by Hollywood riches.

John Green has pointed out that a lot of young people today believe that becoming popular or famous is the end goal of existence today, and there are surely some who approach social media with that very objective. But whatever their individual motives, it can't be denied that today's internet stars are redefining old ways, building new inroads to fame and fortune, new avenues of opportunity, and paving career paths that never existed before.

Discussing his YouTube success in an article on Alex Perry's *Huffington Post* blog, Dan Howell of *Dan & Phil* remarked: "…in terms of finance, skills and career, it's completely changed my life! Prior to YouTube success I was studying Law at the University of Manchester and would probably have been an unhappy solicitor for three years before having an emotional breakdown. YouTube is now my full-time job and has opened the doors to things like BBC Radio 1 and TV and has given me the freedom to do what I want with my life. My future looks very exciting, and I have YouTube and my amazing followers to thank for that."

And speaking to *Women's Wear Daily*, Michelle Phan remarked, "It's kind of crazy to think that six years ago this online community didn't exist."

While the new opportunities being created can be life-changing for some, a few notable YouTubers have stepped out of the spotlight after achieving success as social media stars.

Bertie Gilbert, formerly known by the screenname *bertiebertg*, rose to prominence amid the British social media blitz with funny, charismatic vlogs, which he began posting at age 14. He collaborated with many other noted YouTubers, gaining millions of views and subscribers. However, at the ripe old age of 17, Bertie opted to retire from vlogging, removing his vlog videos from the site. He said that he felt the attention gained from his reputation as a social media personality detracted from his ambitions as a serious filmmaker.

But others have chosen not only to stay, but to expand their social media presence by leaps and bounds, and new internet stars are appearing all the time. It's clearer than ever that social media stardom is still just getting started.

So where it will all lead? Social media is an exciting frontier to watch as the landscape evolves. If you stay tuned to your favorite apps, you will surely witness some interesting history being made as content creators and fans forge ahead together. Who will be the next social media phenom? Toss your hat into the ring, and it could be you. ★